DOWN TO BOWRING'S

A Memoir

© 2015, Derrick Bowring

 Canada Council for the Arts / Conseil des Arts du Canada

 Canada

Newfoundland Labrador

We gratefully acknowledge the financial support of the Canada Council for the Arts, the Government of Canada through the Canada Book Fund (CBF), and the Government of Newfoundland and Labrador through the Department of Tourism, Culture and Recreation for our publishing program.

All rights reserved. No part of this work covered by the copyrights hereon may be reproduced or used in any form or by any means—graphic, electronic or mechanical—without the prior written permission of the publisher. Any requests for photocopying, recording, taping or information storage and retrieval systems of any part of this book shall be directed in writing to the Canadian Reprography Collective, One Yonge Street, Suite 1900, Toronto, Ontario M5E 1E5.

Printed on acid-free paper
Layout by Tracy Harris and Joanne Snook-Hann
Cover design by Todd Manning
Photo restoration by Michael Ripley

Published by
CREATIVE PUBLISHERS
an imprint of CREATIVE BOOK PUBLISHING
a Transcontinental Inc. associated company
P.O. Box 8660, Stn. A
St. John's, Newfoundland and Labrador A1B 3T7

Printed in Canada

Library and Archives Canada Cataloguing in Publication

Bowring, Derrick, 1916-2009, author

    Down to Bowring's : a memoir / Derrick Bowring ; edited by Amy Bowring.

ISBN 978-1-77103-061-8 (paperback)

    1. Bowring (Firm). 2. Bowring, Derrick, 1916-2009. 3. Businesspeople--Newfoundland and Labrador--St. John's--Biography. 4. Department stores--Newfoundland and Labrador--St. John's--History. 5. Family-owned business enterprises--Newfoundland and Labrador--St. John's--History. I. Bowring, Amy, 1971-, editor II. Title.

HF5465.C34B69 2015   381'.141097181   C2015-902138-3

DOWN TO BOWRING'S
A Memoir

Derrick Bowring • Edited by Amy Bowring

St. John's, Newfoundland and Labrador
2015

Captain Basil Gotto's statue "The Fighting Newfoundlander," unveiled on September 13, 1922 in Bowring Park as a memorial to the Newfoundland soldiers who fought in World War I. *Photo: Bruce Templeton*

"This epistle is dedicated to my beloved wife, Gig, whose support and opinions made all the difference, and to Fred Ayre, without whom the growth of the Little Shops would not have happened."

Derrick Bowring

Commemorative bench near the rose garden in Bowring Park donated by the Bowring Park Foundation.
Photo: Bruce Templeton

TABLE OF CONTENTS

Foreword ix

Introduction xi

"The Word" xiii

Chapter One – On the Road to Colinet 1

Chapter Two – Getting Down to Business 7

Chapter Three – Expeditions and Excursions 17

Chapter Four – "Gig" Baird 41

Chapter Five – The Modern Age of Retail 71

Chapter Six – Becoming Canadian 89

Chapter Seven – Extending Branches, Catching Fire 107

Epilogue 139

Bios 141

Sir George Frampton's "Peter Pan," erected in memory of Sir Edgar Bowring's godchild, Betty Munn, who had drowned along with her father when the Florizel sank at Cappahayden. The statue was unveiled on August 29, 1925 with the following inscription, "In memory of a little girl who loved the Park." First commissioned by J.M. Barrie in 1912, seven casts have been made of it and are situated around the world. The original statue is in Kensington Gardens, London, England. *Photo: Bruce Templeton*

FOREWORD

I was more than delighted to be requested by the children of Derrick Bowring to write a foreword to his excellent memoir *Down to Bowring's*.

As Derrick Bowring's fine account shows, soon after Benjamin Bowring came to St. John's in 1811 to establish a business in watch and clock making, he discovered that, if the firm was to prosper, it had to expand its activities to general merchandising and then involve itself in the main economic activities of Newfoundland at that time, which were, of course, the salt cod fishery, the seal fishery and the shipping activities connected with those industries. Benjamin Bowring and his descendants became "Water Street Merchants" and were heavily involved in all of the major economic activities of the colony they had come out to join.

When Derrick arrived from England in 1935 to get involved in the retail side of the business, he immediately liked the life that he discovered in Newfoundland with respect to its outdoor activities and the people themselves. By then Bowring Brothers had grown to be one of the largest merchants in the colony. The cod and seal fisheries, how they operated and contributed to the well-being of the people of Newfoundland, both in the outports and in St. John's, are accurately and well described by the author so that anyone can understand their importance to the overall success of Newfoundland's economy.

Another interesting feature is the author's description of the many changes that took place from his start in the 1930s, through World War II and the coming of Confederation. Derrick describes the modern business methods that were adopted by Bowring's and how the next generation of family members continued to meet changing working conditions. It is interesting to note how the Bowrings participated, with other Newfoundlanders, in supporting the United Kingdom during World War II. And Derrick makes it clear that his success is also attributed to his wife, "Gig", who was his companion for life and a woman of wonderful qualities and of great assistance to him.

I do not have sufficient time or space to do justice to this outstanding family who contributed so much to the economy and life of Newfoundland and also Canada. The Bowring family involved itself in many charitable activities including gifting St. John's with Bowring Park. I congratulate Amy Bowring, Derrick's granddaughter, for editing this first-class memoir of her grandfather, giving us wonderful insights into his life and that of the family history.

I will end by quoting Cicero, the most astute of Roman writers, who wrote in 80 BC that "History is the witness of the times, the torch of truth, the life of memory, the teacher of life, the messenger of antiquity." All of these points are well illustrated in this wonderful, detailed history associated with the coming of the Bowring family and their descendants to the Colony, then Province of Newfoundland. I congratulate the late and very successful Derrick Bowring and all of his descendants and relatives for their wonderful contributions, not only in Newfoundland and Labrador, but in Canada and the U.K. as well. They have also measured up to the virtues that Cicero espouses and which are happily illustrated in this modern Bowring epic.

John Crosbie, PC, OC, ONL, QC
March 2015

INTRODUCTION

I'm not exactly sure when my father decided to dictate his memories, somewhere around 2002, but like his father before him, he was passionately in love with Newfoundland. He was born in Liverpool but grew up in Surrey, England. The tales his father and uncles told excited him enough that when the opportunity came to actually go, he was delighted. The Great Depression was in full flight and job prospects in England were dim. The fact that rain, drizzle and fog would almost do him in due to lifelong asthma would never diminish his affection for the place and, particularly, the people.

Just before he decided to take on the task of creating a memoir, he had been invited by the current owners of Bowring's to cut the ribbon at the opening of one of the last Little Shops, which just happened to be in St. John's. He realized that, having cut the ribbon, he had no control over or connection to the store. In thinking about writing down the history of Bowring Brothers Limited, he is quoted as saying, "If I don't do it, it won't get done. It isn't dull, and if you like history, it's really quite interesting." He felt, rightly so, that the story of Bowring's was a large part of the history of St. John's and that it should not be forgotten. If it was never written down and there was no store here, then Bowring Park would just be a monument to nothing, and it needed to be connected to something.

There are now eight generations of the family descended from Benjamin Bowring, the founder of Bowring's, and I know we cherish the history that has been left to us.

I would like to acknowledge the assistance of so many members of the family who have contributed to Dad's memoir. My siblings, Paula, Vivian and Norman, for their typing skills and memories of dates and many other things. My brothers-in-law, Bruce Templeton and Rob Pallard, for their scanning of old photos and advice in general. My son-in-law Michael Ripley for his talents in photo restoration. Last but not least, my daughter Amy Bowring who, by her knowledge and expertise as a professional historian, editor and published author, was able to guide and encourage her somewhat clueless father on how to proceed to the next step!

Dad's tale is a labour of love for both the family and Newfoundland. Dad, you have indeed left your mark and we will long remember you.

David Bowring, 2014

"THE WORD"

In the beginning was "the word" and the word was "Newfoundland." At least according to Cyril Bowring, my father, who was born in Topsail on October 23rd, 1886. It always surprised me that he was so fond of Newfoundland because he had left the country when he was only three years old after his father died and his mother took the family over to England to educate them. Apart from the first three years of his life, I believe he only visited Newfoundland two or, possibly, three times in the early 1920s when he was working with the family company in New York and from there he paid one or two brief visits in the summer. My father grew up in Liverpool and, after leaving school, he joined the army on August 4th, 1914. In December of that year, he married my mother, also a Liverpudlian, and in due course I appeared in September 1916. My first real memory was at some date in 1919 when my father re-appeared from the war, having spent a large part of it in Egypt and Palestine. In 1919, he was demobilized and on the occasion of his returning to his mother's house, I was invited to ask him if he would like a bottle of Bass, a favourite beer, which he certainly did like.

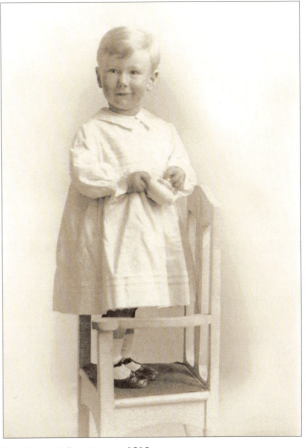

Paul Derrick Bowring, c. 1918

By 1919, I had a brother and in 1920, we all moved to New York where my father was to join Bowring and Company as a director. We lived on Staten Island. I started my education at the local kindergarten and elementary school. In 1925, my father was transferred, at his own request I believe, to C.T. Bowring and Company Limited in London, mainly for the reason that he wanted to educate his children in England. We remained there until I set out on my own to Newfoundland.

Once back in England, I followed the normal course of education for my family, which meant from the ages of nine to 13, a prep school in Westgate-on-Sea, Kent, followed by what was probably one of my most fortunate things, a period at one of the greatest of the public schools – Shrewsbury School in Shropshire. I spent five very enjoyable and instructive years there. I was in the last year of my time at Shrewsbury when I received a visit from my father, totally unexpected and not even on a weekend when I might have been able to go out with him for a meal or two in the town. He arrived, as far as I remember, just after lunch, on an ordinary weekday on which boys would not normally go out with their parents. Regardless, we walked across the campus, down what was called the School Bank to the side of the river – the great Severn River on which the school did a great deal of rowing – then continued along the bank and sat on a bench. I hadn't the foggiest idea why he had come up or what we were doing on our walk. He wasted no time and said there was an opportunity for me with the firm in Newfoundland and would I like to take it. The reason for the offer was that there would be a vacancy in the management of the "shops" division of the business because the present director in charge would be retiring within a few years. It also happened that it was a part of the company that no Bowring had personally shown much interest in, or certainly no knowledge of, and I was to be the first member of the family who would understand what that part of the business was all about. I was 18 at the time and I must admit, I don't think I'd given much thought to what I was going to do in my future life. Equally, I'm sure it didn't take me more than half a minute to reply that yes, I would love to go. Hence this tale.

My father Cyril, mother Clara and my maternal grandparents, Friedrich and Clara Pferdmenges, 1914.

Derrick Bowring, 2002

CHAPTER ONE
ON THE ROAD TO COLINET

While it may be thought that taking a position in Newfoundland was a rash decision, it should be remembered that 1935 was a year in which the world was only just beginning to emerge from the Depression of the 1929 Crash. Unemployment throughout the United Kingdom was colossal; there were very few opportunities that a young man could see as he came to the end of his education. On top of that, I had heard nothing but good about Newfoundland. I knew the family had a company there – what it did I hadn't the foggiest idea, but it seemed to me that whatever it was they did, it was something I would very much like to do.

In those days, one did not automatically think of going to university as you would today, so on August 20th, 1935, I set sail on the great adventure in RMS Newfoundland, the Furness Withy passenger cargo vessel that ran a regular service to St. John's, Halifax and Boston and back to the U.K. I was bringing with me more clothes than I had ever owned in my life, from white tie and tails to black tie and dinner jacket, three or four suits, shirts, socks, shoes, golf clubs and Lord knows what else.

The passengers on the Newfoundland were largely Newfoundlanders returning home from business trips or from holidays, some Canadians on their way to Halifax and perhaps an American or two going to Boston. There were some about my own age. One, a young doctor having just

Last view of the family and England, August 20th, 1935, 7 p.m. My family members are in the centre with my siblings Norman and Sonia looking up at me. My parents are speaking to someone. *Photo: Derrick Bowring*

completed his medical studies in Edinburgh, became a friend for many years to come. Another, slightly younger than me, returning from his time at Lees School, became a close companion and we remained in touch even after the war when he married an American and went to live and work in the United States. He became our eldest daughter's godfather and, in the years to come, we attended the various weddings of all our children. I realized that many of the Newfoundland passengers recognized my name but had no idea why I was on the boat and assumed that I was coming out for a holiday in St. John's with my uncle, which was what many people used to do. They had no idea that I was out as a permanent fixture.

We had a rather rough passage, which took seven days instead of the normal five and a half. A day or two before our arrival, I received a radiogram from my Uncle Eric in St. John's, telling me to hurry up because as soon as I arrived, we were to go on a camping trip. In fact, we arrived at 2 or 3 a.m. when I was still in my bunk and I never saw the spectacular picture of St. John's as a vessel enters The Narrows. Fortunately, my uncle was on the dockside to meet me at a reasonably civilized hour. If he hadn't done so, I don't really know what I would have done. I was barely aware of the company I was going to work for and I certainly hadn't the slightest idea where my uncle lived. Anyway, it all passed off well – we loaded my hand luggage, left the trunk and golf clubs to be brought out later by one of Bowring Brothers' vans, set off through St. John's, and out the Portugal Cove Road to his summer residence at Murray's Pond which, because of its mansard roof, was fondly know as the "Mushroom." It was a lovely summer's day; the sun was shining and Newfoundland looked at its absolute best, especially the landscapes that were unfamiliar – the beautiful blue of Twenty Mile Pond that we drove past on the way to Murray's Pond. I learned on the way that in Newfoundland, every piece of fresh water was known as a pond. It didn't matter how big it was, how many square miles it covered, it was always a pond.

As soon as I arrived at the "Mushroom" I was told that we were about to depart on our camping trip and would I kindly assemble whatever other equipment I might need for a five-day trip living under canvas. The party for the camping trip consisted of my uncle, his daughters Joan and Lorna (known as Pix), my uncle's sister-in-law, and a neighbour at Murray's Pond called Fred Ayre who was known to me from Shrewsbury because we were there at the same time and were approximately the same age. Fred was a little older and, from time to time, we had found ourselves in the same form learning the same German or French. My cousins were also well known to me since they had been at school in England. As they only came back to Newfoundland for the summer holidays, they frequently spent the Christmas and Easter holidays with my parents in Merstham in the south of England. My uncle's sister-in-law, Edie Winter, was a widow. Her husband had been a great friend of my uncle's and she was kindness itself the first winter I spent in Newfoundland.

The camping party travelled in two vehicles, one a very new Rover that suffered from the problem of being very low to the ground, which was not what you needed on the Newfoundland roads of the day. Therefore, it could only be driven by my uncle who treated it with great caution and nobody else was allowed near it except as passengers. The other vehicle was what was known as a Humber Touring Car. It had a canvas roof that could fold down and it had "gate" gears, essentially a complex clutch system. It was the type of vehicle on which I had learned to drive a couple of years earlier. The Rover could only carry a modest load but the Humber was like a truck and it carried the tent, which was a monstrous affair, plus a pile of food, whatever clothing we carried and anything else that was needed for the camping trip. In 1935 there were only two paved roads in the St. John's area: one from St. John's to Portugal Cove, on which Murray's Pond was situated; and the Topsail Road from the west end of St. John's out to Conception Bay, where Topsail was situated. This was paved as far as Manuels River, which was a couple miles beyond Topsail. Everything else was gravel road maintained by a series of section men who were equipped with a horse, a box cart and a wooden contraption that could be used to grade the road after the section man had filled in the potholes with gravel. Gravel was no problem – Newfoundland seemed to be solid rock. So off we went from the "Mushroom" back into St. John's for some supplies that hadn't yet been obtained. We stopped outside the Bowring stores but did not go in, obtained what we needed and carried on until we arrived in Topsail, then onto Manuels. Here we stopped for some homemade ice cream at a little store run by Peter Butler. After crossing the Manuels bridge, we were then on the gravel and we remained on the gravel until we returned to Manuels a few days later.

We drove on in the direction of Salmonier, which took us along the coast of Conception Bay South to Holyrood. I was quite struck by scenery that was, in many ways, quite different from my home in England – grey slate rock, masses of evergreens and so many ponds and lakes dotting the landscape. We reached Salmonier and called in on the Murrays, another St. John's merchant family, who had a summer place on the Salmonier River, which lived up to its name as a very good salmon-fishing river. After a short stop there, we carried on in the direction of Colinet, with the next plan being to select a campground and generally get ourselves organized for the first night. We found a very suitable flat, clear area with plenty of room for the tent and fire, and with suitable trees within easy reach that could be cut down, limbed and generally prepared to hold the tent up. Though undoubtedly a horrifying prospect to 21st-century campers and environmentalists, 1930s camping technology required one to use found or acquired branches to support the tent. The leave-no-trace philosophy of camping did not emerge until the 1960s. The tent needed at least five trees cut down and limbed, which was done with a bucksaw and the two axes that were carried in the Humber. It was a square type of building and, when properly erected, was very roomy with lots of headroom. We finished the construction by using all the limbs that had been taken off the tree trunks to make what was known as a bough bed and, though rugged, it proved to be very comfortable during our first night there. My first night in Newfoundland was spent under canvas on the road to Colinet.

We did our cooking on a great big fire that today would get you locked up in pretty quick order. While we were careful with the fire, not allowing it to get out of hand and with water from a nearby stream available to take care of any problems, it still was a magnificent blaze that we kept going during the evening to ward off the flies and to provide a bit of cheer. Looking back, I wonder how we managed to get away with it. Mark you, no one passed on the road during the whole time we were there and in the morning we packed everything up, re-loaded the cars and set off for our next destination.

Our next port of call was Placentia, the old French capital of Newfoundland, which boasted two hotels. We spent our second night at Fulford's Hotel by the side of the Southeast Arm. Fulford's Hotel in Placentia was run by a Mrs. Fulford and her husband Ned. Mrs. Fulford was many years older than her husband and the story goes that as she was leaving the church after the marriage to her first husband, Ned, still an infant, was being carried in to be baptized. By the time I encountered them, Mrs. Fulford had married Ned; she ran the hotel and Ned was the guide for salmon fishing and general dog's body around the hotel. In fact, when milk was required for a meal, Ned would be sent out with a bucket to obtain it from their cow. The milk was therefore warm. The menu for meals at Fulford's was reputed to be limited so on one day you could have ham or lamb, and the next day you could have lamb or ham. Nevertheless, it was a pleasant place for us to spend a night and part of a day. To me it was a real experience of things to come.

The next day we drove down the Cape Shore as far as Gooseberry, which had a beautiful sandy beach where we relaxed in the sun for a short period, had a picnic lunch, came back over our tracks and took the road through Markland and on to Whitbourne. Somewhere in that area we pitched our second camp, re-erected the tent and went through all the motions of surviving another night. On the following day we packed everything aboard the cars and drove up the road on the south side of Trinity Bay as far as Heart's Content. There we spent the night in the local boarding house, which was really very comfortable. The following day we drove over what were known as the Heart's Content Barrens to Carbonear. The route then went along the shore road on the north side of Conception Bay back to Holyrood where we joined the road that we had previously taken near the beginning of our trip and from there it was back to the "Mushroom." Thus ended my first four nights in Newfoundland and very enjoyable it was, with beautiful August summer weather and pleasant company. I thought I'd arrived in Paradise.

I had about a week or 10 days at the "Mushroom" where my helpful cousins introduced me to a great number of the local youth and beauty and where we enjoyed tennis, rowing

Uncle Eric's White Knight, seen here in 1937, provided many wonderful hours of leisure over the years.

on the pond and several parties, which in the summer were quite frequent. They were all private parties and the very first one I attended was hosted by people I didn't know. In fact, I don't think I ever really learned who was giving the party. It was in a private house and there I met a lot of people whose names I found hard to remember because there were so many of them. This particular party was being given for a pair of cousins by one of their fathers. While the father and his son were present, his niece was not. She worked at the Bank of Montreal and when it came to the end of the month, whatever books had to be balanced, had to be balanced even if it meant being at work until midnight or later. While her own party raged on in her uncle's house, she was down at the Bank of Montreal on Water Street, trying to balance the books. It was only some considerable time later that I discovered the party was for her and her cousin – the absent niece would later become my wife.

CHAPTER TWO
GETTING DOWN TO BUSINESS

At last, along came the day when I was due to start my apprenticeship at Bowring Brothers. September 15th, 1935 – it got off to a good start, but ended in a bit of an anticlimax. My mentor for the period of my training was to be a delightful old gentleman called Walter Woodman Wills – three initials, W.W.W., that I came to know well over the next five or six years. Unfortunately, I was deposited in the office by my uncle who discovered that Walter Wills was still on his holidays and wouldn't be back for several more days. However, the problem of what to do with me for the time being was solved by putting me into the cage with the two company cashiers.

At that time, there were very few mechanical aids to office work. Adding machines existed but they were very rare. There were also calculators but they were even more cumbersome and it was quicker to do the arithmetic in your head. All cheques were written out by one of the two cashiers according to orders issued by the appropriate bookkeepers. The cheques were then taken and signed by one of the directors who had signing authority. Wages were paid in cash and this meant that once a week the payroll had to be assembled in the right amount of currency, which was then sorted according to how much each man or woman was to receive in a little envelope with their name on it. This was then distributed to the department managers who in turn, handed them out to the appropriate individuals. I'm sure I was thoroughly in the way of the two elderly gents who ran the cash department but they were very pleasant and agreeable people with a good sense of humour. They thought it was rather

Eric A. Bowring, c. 1950.

A colleague we called "Mac," Walter Wills and I, Bowring's northside wharf, 1937.

fun to have a junior Bowring in the cage with them who was supposedly "assisting" them in work that they could do far more quickly if left on their own. By the following Monday, Walter had returned to the office and my real training commenced.

Since there were to be two of us in the same office, we needed to have a double desk instead of the single one that Walter had used up to that time. I was so ignorant of what went on in an office and who paid for what that I was gravely worried at one point that I would have to pay for half the desk, and there was also an element of doubt as to how much I was actually going to be paid. Before I left England, my father had told me that I was to receive $1,500 a year. Well, since I was accustomed to pounds, shillings and pence, the number of dollars really meant very little to me and $1,500 sounded like a lot of money. I was perfectly satisfied with it. However, soon after I had arrived, my uncle told me that I was not going to receive $1,500 but rather $500 or $40 a month. Even that, at the beginning, didn't register very highly but I was acutely aware that my pay had been cut by two-thirds. My uncle also said the problem would partially be solved by the fact that I could live with him and I wouldn't have to pay board and the remaining $500 would have to do me pretty well as pocket money for my entertainments or other jollifications.

The cause of the change in salary was based on the objections of an older generation relation who was a senior director in London. He wasn't even a Bowring, he was a Stoddart and the Stoddarts were descended through a Bowring daughter who had naturally taken her husband's name. However, all of them had Bowring as their second name, such as Laurence Bowring Stoddart, George Bowring Stoddart, and so on. Most of them looked to the firm to give them jobs. Some of them were quite serious shareholders as was this one, Laurence Stoddart.

Laurence Stoddart had started his career with the firm, I think in New York, as an apprentice. He had spent perhaps a year or more attached to Bowring Brothers in Newfoundland, which he didn't like, and they didn't like him much either. He was there in the very early 1900s and since he was paid $500 a year, he didn't see why another generation, 30 or more years later, after a World War with enormous inflation, should be paid any more than he had received. Since his contemporaries didn't think it worth arguing about, I got cut

Bowring Brothers' sealing fleet: SS Kite, Bktn Imogene, SS Algerine, SS Terra Nova, SS Aurora, Schr Lottie, 1899. *Photo: James Vey*

back to $500. I must admit that I used this, what I considered pretty shabby treatment, to get my own back on him later.

When I first met Walter Wills, he was in his late 60s but had been with the company since his teens. It was his first job and he had worked his way up through the ranks to third director and he was the one in charge of what were known as the "shops." Prior to becoming a director, he had been the manager of one of the major departments of the retail store. It was the only department that didn't sell anything at retail but sold everything wholesale – a little peculiarity that I found Newfoundland to be full of. Walter had always been very conscious of the need to control credit and he had an extensive knowledge of outport business and the soundness of various merchants whom we supplied, so that when they wanted somebody with knowledge of the trading business, he was invited to join the board. The reason that I had been given the opportunity to join the company was because the board of directors wanted to have one member of the family who understood the detailed working of the "shops" since they were the best moneymakers. All other family members were more interested in sealing, fish and shipping – in other words, the gambling side.

Bowring Brothers had started life in 1811 when Benjamin Bowring came out to St. John's to establish his business of watch and clock making, which had been his trade in Exeter, Devon. The business first operated under his own name, later to become Benjamin Bowring and Sons after his wife and sons had joined him in St. John's. After his retirement and the sons took over, it became Bowring Brothers. That was in 1841. Benjamin Bowring's retirement to Liverpool seems to have been more nominal than factual as, for many years, he continued to assist as purchasing agent and forwarder of goods that he arranged to purchase for the firm and ship out by a variety of vessels. He also obviously took a considerable interest in the business and offered many comments to his sons in St. John's as to the suitability of vessels for their various requirements. His second son, Charles Tricks Bowring, later joined him in Liverpool and established his own company, C.T. Bowring and Company, which later became the parent company of the entire group. As soon as the British Companies Act came into force in 1899, C.T. Bowring and Company became a limited liability company. Shortly thereafter, when the Newfoundland Companies Act was passed, Bowring Brothers again was incorporated. The main shareholder was C.T. Bowring and Company Limited and since the shareholders of C.T. Bowring and Company and the partners of Bowring Brothers in St. John's were all the same people, C.T. Bowring and Company became the virtual owner of Bowring Brothers Limited.

After he emigrated in 1811, Benjamin Bowring soon found that watch making alone would not be enough and his store soon added additional lines of considerable variety. Eventually, he found himself trading in general merchandise and became part of the Newfoundland economy. This was mainly the cod fishery, followed by the seal fishery and products related to both. He and his sons became Water Street merchants. When I appeared as a fifth-generation member, I was painted with the same brush. Water Street merchants have been labelled everything from the main cause of Newfoundland's troubles of every kind, to the saviours of the economy, according to one's point of view. In fact, they range from one extreme to the other as with any group of human beings. Some were as honest as the day is long and some were not. All of them had to endure a fickle and narrowly based economy that flourished in wartime and struggled in peace. Everything depended on the price of fish as well as the quantity thereof. The initial tenets instilled in me were that honesty and integrity were the two most important words in business and don't you forget them. I never did.

In 1935, Bowring Brothers operated from three premises in St. John's. The main site was the Water Street one where the buildings spanned a 120-foot frontage on the south side

Bowring Brothers' Northside Premises, c. 1936.

Bowring Brothers' Southside Premises for unloading, canning and packing fish, c. 1936.

of Water Street bounded on the west by Beck's Cove, and on the east by the Pitts Building, which was a competitive retailer operated by Ayre and Sons. The southern exposure was on the waterfront where there were three wooden finger piers used for visiting schooners and for the outfitting of vessels for the seal fishery. The second premises were on the south side of the harbour, roughly midway from east to west, and it was from here that the seal fishery and the processing of the resulting catch was carried out and where the handling of cod oil and shipment for export took place. The third premises were at the west end of the harbour, close to the dry-dock and were known as Mudge's Premises, but which, in fact, belonged to the British Admiralty from whom Bowring Brothers rented them. This was where the salt codfish was handled. It was received, culled, weighed, packed and then shipped for export.

At the time, the company owned five sealing vessels including the Imogene, which was the only sealing vessel actually built for the purpose. All other vessels were either converted whaling ships or cargo boats that were reinforced to handle ice. The company's fleet included the Beothic, which was a First World War cargo boat strengthened for ice; the Terra Nova, a wooden ex-whaler whose claim to fame was that she had carried the Scott Expedition to the South Pole in 1912; the Eagle, which was also a wooden vessel; and the Ranger, another converted whaler. They spent most of their time tied up at the Southside since they were really of no value in general cargo carrying, being too expensive to operate compared to the revenue they could generate based on the amount of cargo each could carry.

The Water Street buildings contained the retail shops, which fronted onto Water Street, and the General Office, which was situated on the south side of the building, overlooking the finger piers and the harbour. On the Beck's Cove side was a separate building known as

SS Eagle, SS Terra Nova and SS Ranger at the Southside Premises, c. 1936.

the retail store even though it sold its merchandise solely at wholesale. The Water Street stores consisted of 11 buildings cobbled together forming separate shops. They contained a department known as dry goods, which was located at the east end of the building. There was a fashion department, a hardware department and a retail grocery. Each department was presided over by a department manager; they virtually had little kingdoms with very limited interference from anybody except when matters pertained to the granting of credit and the standards of employment and wages that were relatively common throughout the business.

The manager of the fashion department was the only woman in a management position and she answered to the dry goods manager even though, as a department manager himself, he was essentially her equal in terms of the level of management. In charge of these four managers was Walter W. Wills, the director in charge of the shops who himself had been a department manager of the retail store. In fact, the retail store, as I found it, had been built during his period of management and was fairly new. Because he had been a department manager in his earlier days, he was very conscious of the fact that each manager must be able to run his department without interference from anybody else. Only very reluctantly would he put his oar into something that should or should not be done during the regular run of trading. He did control the credit that could be granted and was aided by a credit manager who worked in the general office. The four managers had very independent commands and it was something that I found somewhat difficult at a later stage in my career.

Within the General Office of the Water Street building, were three very pleasant offices, one each for the resident directors, and in one of them, I wound up with Walter Wills. The other two were occupied by my uncle, who was the managing director, and the middle one by Edgar Bowring Jr., who was the middle ranking director. I discovered that the managing director was known as the Skipper, the second Bowring was known as the Boss and that took care of the family. The rest of the office came straight out of a Dickens novel. It consisted of eight huge ledgers, each with its own bookkeeper situated on the stand-up, high desks that were fashionable in the Victorian era. There was also the credit manager who had a separate office and another office full of typists who were attached to the credit department. In the corner, there was a cage that had two very senior people, the chief cashier and the second cashier. There was a chief accountant who was in charge of the whole process of bookkeeping and accounting and he had an assistant who actually wrote up the general ledger, which was the final word on what we had succeeded in doing. There was the second ledger with the next senior bookkeeper and the third, fourth, fifth and sixth, all in ranking order. The fifth and sixth ledgers contained, mainly, the accounts of retail customers of the Water Street store. The third and fourth ledgers were, essentially, wholesale dealers around the entire country. The second one was mainly

A Bowring Brothers' horse and cart participating in a parade along Military Road, 1936.

concerned with the sealing, fish trading and cod oil trading. The number one ledger or general ledger was, of course, the collecting point for all of this information.

There was a lot for me to learn. I had never, except in reading novels, met a ledger face to face and I hadn't the foggiest idea about what was then called "double entry bookkeeping". The most I could imagine was a sort of cash account keeping track of a bit of money in your pocket if you wanted to make a note of what you had done with it. It took me a long time to get double entry bookkeeping straight in my mind, which simply illustrates that one shouldn't go into business directly out of school when you have never heard of any of these things. I remember at one point wondering why on earth a company had to account for depreciation. It seemed to me that if you had bought, say, a truck and had spent the money on it, why did you have to pay for it all over again through depreciation? However, in the end I did learn and I did understand and I participated in the process quite happily from then on.

I discovered how the retail departments were operated by spending time in them each day, partly with the appropriate manager, partly with various members of the staff. Of course, in doing so I got to know the individuals themselves who were, I must admit, a most delightful lot, full of good humour and all most loyal employees of the company. At first, I naturally assumed that every task was being done in the best possible way of achieving the required result, and I accepted everything more or less at face value. It was only after a period of some years that I began to question certain methods. Over time, I gave much thought to the best way to run a retail department store, never mind the wholesale side, which I rapidly came to believe was not one with any great future to it. The more I learned, the more I felt that the wholesale business contained too much risk with so much credit being given; the future, it seemed to me, lent itself better to the retail stores.

Part of my training had to take into account the other activities of the company and I remember one occasion where my uncle decided that as part of the learning process about the fish business, I should make a study of the ledgers that dealt with our participation in the cod fishery for a period of 50 years and work out the gains and losses over that period and see how it all stood in the aggregate. Each year had its own massive Dickensian-styled ledger, which had to be dug out of the vaults. Slightly unwillingly at first, because it seemed a monumental labour about something that was so old as to be irrelevant, I worked my way through it; I did it both for codfish and cod oil and I began to see that there was a distinct pattern, and the figures themselves became more interesting. In the end, having taken each year individually over this 50-year period and totted up the gains and losses, I discovered that we had done all this activity for a very substantial loss over a half century. When I presented my uncle with my final figures, showing the year-by-year result plus the aggregate final loss, I posed the question to him: since we didn't seem able to make any money dealing in codfish, why didn't we get out of the business and stick to the things that made money? He had an immediate reply. He said we cannot give up handling codfish. It is the currency of the colony. In other words, somebody has to take the fish from the fishermen or from the outport dealer and process it and pack it and sell it in the world market because the fisherman himself cannot do that. Most outport dealers are not big enough to be able to cope and that brings it right back to the poor benighted Water Street merchant who is going to get blamed in the end for whatever goes wrong.

CHAPTER THREE
EXPEDITIONS AND EXCURSIONS

In May of 1936, I set out on Newfoundland's railway line to visit a fairly large number of wholesale customers who lived within reach of the railway; my guide and mentor was Heber Harnett, one of the dry goods salesmen who travelled for the company. He specialized in the communities that could be reached by rail and there was another wholesale traveller who covered the south coast and the east coast, which could only be reached by the regular coastal boat service operated by the Newfoundland Government. Heber Harnett was a most enjoyable companion and was well able to guide my footsteps as to how to deal with and treat the various people I was to meet, all of whom, of course, were complete strangers to me, as I was to them.

We set off from St. John's on what was known as the Express, which at that time of the year probably ran twice a week from St. John's, up along the northern coast to the west side of the island, then south to Port aux Basques, and then return. In the summer the frequency was increased. It was a new experience for me; in England, trains from the village in which I lived ran up to London with a frequency of about one every half hour.

We had sleepers for the first stage because we were not going to leave the train until about seven o'clock the following morning when we were to arrive at Bishop's Falls. This was a railway junction northeast of Grand Falls and there we disembarked for Botwood, which was the port for shipping the products of the paper mill at Grand Falls by steamer to the United Kingdom. The paper mill was owned by the Anglo-Newfoundland Development Company (AND), which in turn belonged to the Northcliff Press, publishers of the *Daily Mail*, etc. We left the train complete with about six monumental wicker hampers of dry goods samples that were then loaded on a truck and Heber and I joined the driver in the cab and set off for Botwood. In Botwood, we rented a small hall for the display of the samples and we found accommodation at the Argyle Hotel. This was an experience in itself for the plumbing arrangements at the Argyle Hotel, which was a nice, commodious building, were based on a privy out on the grounds and the guests would have to wend their way when nature needed relieving. I hadn't encountered that before.

From Botwood, we returned by our truck to Bishop's Falls where the samples were displayed all over again. I can assure you that unpacking and displaying five or six hamper loads of samples and repacking them after each visit is quite a sizable task. We set up shop in Bishop's Falls and local merchants came to view the samples; Heber then took their orders, which were dispatched by mail to St. John's as we went on to the next port of call.

Heber had an approved list of accounts whose credit was good and who could be sold merchandise; he also had a list with sundry warnings such as "don't overdo it with so-and-so" and, above all, "don't take an order from somebody else who was a bit behind with his payments." I was quite surprised and so was Heber Harnett, to discover that through my participation in the opening of the mail and the consideration of the various companies and their need for credit, that I had, over five or six months, picked up quite a lot of knowledge of which I was not even conscious until I started meeting the customers concerned.

From Bishop's Falls, we mounted the express train again and, to my surprise, went well to the west side of the island to a little place called Robinsons, which had one account with whom we dealt and Heber thought it was worth a stop. I think he also thought that I would enjoy Robinsons because it was on the coast. There were glorious sandy beaches and we might be able to catch a few fish. We spent two or three pleasant days in Robinsons and then, as far as I can remember, took a return train back to Corner Brook, which we had passed on our way out.

Corner Brook led to my first argument with Heber Harnett because he contended that all the worthwhile accounts were on what was called Corner Brook West. The decent hotel run by the paper company was on the east side, the main part of Corner Brook proper, which had a fine modern supply of plumbing that I was determined to avail of as I reckoned I was in need of an honest-to-God bath. So, reluctantly, Heber, who didn't think I was fit to be let loose on my own, came to stay at the Glynmill Inn as well. I noticed that on subsequent trips that he made without me, he continued to stay at the Glynmill Inn, never mind that all the accounts were over at Corner Brook West. While in Corner Brook, I was given a tour of the paper mill, a truly massive enterprise that was of enormous value through the employment it provided; it really was the main engine that kept the whole economy moving on the west side of the island. I also had my first ride on what was known as a "speeder," a sort of four-wheel bogey. It had a small, gas-powered engine and you put the speeder on the railway line, and when there were no trains coming, off you went to wherever the track took you. I was in the company of another man who was a Junior Forest Warden visiting Corner Brook and he and I and the driver of the speeder set off for St. George's where there are the most beautiful sandy beaches. I'm not sure what my companion was going there for but in any event it was an enjoyable trip out in the open air, and May in Newfoundland is not always that warm. I suppose we covered about 40 miles going there and back and we did it in perfect safety. We never met another train or anything else on the way there or on our return.

Heber and I continued our journey making many stops, including Badger, at about three o'clock in the morning. We had travelled there in the caboose of an ore train heading for Botwood that had come up onto the main line from Buchans where the ore had been mined. Three o'clock in the morning is not the best time for booking into hotels and anyway, Badger didn't have a hotel – it had one or two boarding houses and it also had an AND Company staff house, though not at three o'clock in the morning. However, Heber and I went to what he described as a good boarding house and, on our arrival, we discovered there was one bedroom with one double bed, and into it, we pitched. The room was also occupied by several thousand enormous mosquitoes and I think I spent the rest of the night, while Heber snored, swatting them on the walls so that the room was re-decorated by the time we got up. I suppose I had some sleep. Anyway, I objected to the arrangement and Heber promised to see what he could do about the staff house. If a room was even available, I would need the agreement of the AND Company manager. He was the woods manager of the AND Company and was the king of Badger. There was an available room and the woods manager was agreeable that I should have it and there I went in considerable comfort. I met one of my companions who had come on the boat from England with me, a recently graduated doctor called Arthur Knowling who was the resident doctor employed by the AND Company for that area of their operations; we had an entertaining reunion. Another little sidelight on that visit is that the AND Company woods manager, whom I met for the first time, turned out to be Hugh Cole, the father of my future brother-in-law, Harvey Cole.

There's a good story about Hugh Cole and a wasp's nest though I wasn't present when this event happened. You have to know that Hugh Cole needed two five-foot tape measures to encompass his girth and he was relatively short to go with it. It appeared that there was a wasp's nest under the eaves of his house and the local doctor suggested a solution using his supply of chloroform. If they soaked some cotton wool in the chloroform and poked it into the nest, that ought to deal with the wasps. A small group assembled for this attempt and the chloroform was thrust into the wasps' nest. This naturally produced a cloud of wasps hastening to get away from the fumes. The two-legged party took off down the main street of Badger at the highest speed they could maintain, which left Hugh Cole decidedly in the rear. He shortly discovered that he had a wasp in his pants so he stopped, removed the pants, and presumably the wasp, and then carried on at his best speed down the main street of Badger. History never related what happened thereafter or if the wasps ever disappeared from the poor man's eaves.

Other places visited on the railway trip included Harry's River, Norris Arm, the Port au Port Peninsula on the west coast. After a total of about six weeks, we returned to St. John's. The wholesale sales trips were carried out by other salesmen selling hardware, for example, on the railway line and dry goods travelling salesmen went on the coastal boats for the south and east coasts. The amount of capital required to cope with the credit extended for these wholesale sales was really quite extraordinary and out of all proportion to the value of the business. I did not appreciate this fact at the time, of course, but as the years went by and

I finally became more responsible for the activities of the company, they were very much a deciding factor in the changes we made.

In the spring of 1937 came my trip to the seal hunt on board SS Imogene, the one and only sealing vessel that was actually built for the job. Constructed in 1929, she was relatively young compared to the other vessels of the fleet. The Imogene was a steel vessel, built as an icebreaker in that she had a rounded bow that was capable of riding up on the pans of ice and her resulting weight would break the pan. She also had what was called a long run aft, which enabled pans of ice that had been tilted on end to travel aft and level themselves out again before the tilted pan managed to knock a blade off the propeller – a fatal mistake. The other steel vessel in the fleet was the Beothic, built in 1918 as an American wartime Liberty ship. She had been strengthened for ice and was a good carrier of seals if she was able to actually get to the patch. The remaining ships were the old "wooden walls," the most famous of which was the Terra Nova, built in 1884, which achieved its fame by being the vessel that carried the Scott Expedition to the Antarctic in 1912. Built of oak in Dundee, Scotland, she was much the same in 1937 as she had been in 1912 and the wardroom was the way it appeared and was used in Scott's time at the South Pole. Dating back to 1872 and also an oak ship from Dundee, was the Ranger, the oldest and smallest vessel in the fleet.

The SS Imogene in profile showing her rounded bow, 1937.

She was being sent for her annual sealing trip to the Gulf of St. Lawrence. I never discovered exactly why, but for the whole of my sealing time with the company that's where she went. She was quite successful on her own. Then there was the Norwegian-built vessel Eagle, from 1902, which was constructed of pine, but like all the other wooden vessels, sheaved with greenheart to take the wear and tear of passing through ice. The Ranger was 500 tons and relatively low powered, although quite good in ice; the Terra Nova was 764 tons; the Eagle, 677 tons.

When the seal fishery was due to begin, there was a great deal of activity in preparing the five boats for the voyage. They were brought from their mooring spots to the north side finger piers. The Ranger was brought in first as she would be leaving before the others because she had further to travel to get to the ice fields of the Gulf of St. Lawrence. The Imogene could be poked in bow first toward the office building with the Terra Nova on the other side of the same wharf. The Beothic was berthed at the Southside Premises since she was too large to fit between the finger piers, and the Eagle would come over to the north side after the Ranger had departed for the Gulf. Bowring Brothers had been involved in the seal fishery for so long that there were standard lists of all the equipment and food and other supplies that had to be provided for each ship and the work was divided into different responsibilities. For example, the engine room supplies were the responsibility of the chief engineer and each vessel had a permanently employed chief engineer to look after the supplies and to employ the additional engineers who were required for the sealing voyage. There was a marine superintendent over all the engineers and it was up to him to see that each vessel had its full requirement of safety gear and similar equipment. He also had the help of the bosun of each ship who was another permanent employee. On the feeding side, there was a full-time chief steward who was in charge of the food list and provisions, including the cooking gear. The food itself was provided from either the grocery department or the retail store (which only sold wholesale!). The director who was in charge of the seal fishery overall looked after the supply of bunker coal. This was a considerable quantity as each vessel was totally filled, apart from space for the crew, with coal bunkers, including the holds that would eventually be filled with seal pelts. The coal would usually be ordered from Wales, which provided the type of coal the sealing captains preferred because it burned with a cleaner flame and caused less black "giveaway" smoke, so that other vessels could not see what their competitors were up to. This would be brought out to St. John's in a chartered vessel some time before the start of the seal fishery and be transferred from the carrier to each sealing vessel by a large group of longshoremen. Walter Wills was the one who really looked after the detail of the small supplies that were under the control of the bosun, the steward or the chief cook of each ship. He would have each bosun up to his office with the appropriate list for the vessel and go over it with them item by item. Did he have it, did he have the right number, were they good quality, etc? They included such things as the wooden gaffs that each sealer had to have, the tow ropes that he would need to haul seal pelts and all kinds of little items that, without a list upon which to check them, were likely to have been forgotten. This was Walter's major work – seal fishery outfitting. He did the same with the chief steward and with the equivalent man on each vessel with regard to food, kettles, pots and pans and other paraphernalia that was needed to see that everybody was fed properly. It was really quite a time-consuming but very necessary activity.

The seal fishery was conducted under the rules of the Sealing Act of the Newfoundland House of Assembly, which had been in existence since 1916. Among various safety, quota and labour regulations, it also provided the date at which the first taking of seals could happen and a closing date at the other end of the calendar. These dates determined the launch date for vessels so they could sail before what was called the killing date in order to have sufficient time to get to the front or to the Gulf and to actually discover where the main seal patch was located, because it could be in any number of spots on the vast Atlantic Ocean that bordered the island of Newfoundland. Consequently, we were due to sail for the front on March 6th, which would give us a week in which to search for the seals and get ourselves actually into the patch proper before the killing date. However, on March 2nd there came a call from a ship named the SS Esmond, which belonged to the Anglo-Newfoundland Development Company whose paper operations were in Grand Falls. She had been in ice, not far from Cape Race, and in trying to pass through it had knocked a blade off her propeller and now was in need of a tow to St. John's, where she was due to load paper. The Imogene, being ready for sea and equipped with engineers, stokers, cooks and a navigator, was able to leave immediately to effect the salvage operation and because I was also ready to embark on my sealing adventure, I went along for the ride. This proved to be an extremely interesting and enjoyable experience. We sailed from St. John's in the daylight and set course for Cape Race, some 69 miles away. It soon became dark and we expected to arrive at the Esmond's position and attach the towing cable at first light the following morning. Travelling south in the dark at that time of year is interesting because there are always a number of icebergs floating south and it's possible to see them reflected, even in the dark, in some sort of illumination from the north. We had to be far more cautious when returning with the Esmond in tow, because icebergs disappear in the darkness when you are northbound.

We arrived early the following morning and the captain stopped the ship close to the Esmond. There was a very calm ocean so both vessels were very close to one another, almost within shouting distance. The Imogene's captain went over to the Esmond with the aid of a dory. The ice the Esmond was in was not very heavy and it was easy to manoeuvre. The two captains conferred on the best way of arranging the tow and it was decided that the Imogene would tow the Esmond using the Esmond's chain cable after the anchor had been removed

Top Left: Imogene approaching the Esmond to take line on board. Top Right: First light line coming aboard Imogene from the Esmond. Middle Left: Esmond paying out anchor chain as the tow commences. Bottom Right: Esmond being towed to St. John's. Bottom Left: Imogene bringing the Esmond through the Narrows with tugs attached to the Esmond's stern to slow her down. *Photos: Derrick Bowring*

and this would provide sufficient weight that the tow was unlikely to become taut as the two vessels separated. As the Imogene started to move ahead, the Esmond would pay out the chain until there was sufficient distance between the vessels and then the chain would be made fast on the Esmond's windlass and both vessels would move slowly and surely towards St. John's. The chief engineer of the Imogene took charge of fastening the end of the chain on board the Imogene and it was very interesting to see how this was achieved. The Imogene was not an ocean going tug and not equipped with a towing winch or even bollards for towing purposes. In order to make everything fast, so that there would be no slippage or even breakage, several of her after bollards had to be used and even one wire cable was led from the end of the chain around her after hatch combings and back to the chain via one or two bollards on the way. There was very little chance that the two ships would become separated under virtually any circumstance other than human releasing of the fixings.

The Esmond's captain thought that we might tow her at perhaps three knots, but the Imogene was a powerful ship, quite capable of 15 knots on her own, and once we got the Esmond underway, we managed to tow her at about six knots, heading north for St. John's. By the time everything had been put together and we actually got underway, it was apparent that it would be early the morning of the following day before we would be off the entrance to the Narrows and, since the Esmond had no method of stopping herself, other than simply running ahead until she ran out of momentum, the Imogene's captain signalled Bowring's office in St. John's to ask for the two harbour steam tugs to meet us outside the Narrows so that they could be attached to the stern of the Esmond as we came through the Narrows. We could not idle our way through as we had to maintain steerage way on both Imogene and Esmond, and the idea of the tugs was that they would slow her down once we were in the harbour and she could then be manoeuvred alongside one of the steamship wharves. Everything went according to plan. It was a windless morning and both vessels came through the Narrows without any trouble. The tugs slowed the Esmond down and brought her to a stop and then pushed her alongside one of Harvey's wharves. The Imogene returned to her own berth at our finger pier and tidied up the commotion on her afterdeck.

The one interesting thing that was quite important in relation to the salvage award was the fact that I had taken a camera with me as I had it ready to take to the seal fishery. It seemed that this sort of salvage would lend itself to some interesting photographs. I took a couple of rolls of film and photographed each stage of the proceedings, from the captain going to the Esmond, the lashing of the cable to the aft end of the Imogene, to the tow getting underway and, above all, the ice that was surrounding the Esmond when we arrived and through which the Imogene towed her. I took more photos of the tow and our passage through the Narrows with the tugs on the stern. When the photographs were developed and enlarged, they formed part of the claim for salvage that we forwarded to the insurance

This photo was taken by Walter Wills, and on the back he wrote, "Imogene backing out from the Northside Premises for the seal fishery March 6th 8 a.m., and there goes Derrick on his holiday. W.W.W." Note the sealers waiting to board the next ship in line.

company, Lloyd's of London, since the job was done under what was known as the Lloyd's Open Form. This enables two captains, the one in trouble and the one doing the salvage, to get on with the job, each of them agreeing that the salvage award will be adjudicated by a committee appointed by Lloyd's. They would weigh up the degree of difficulty and the values involved. The photographs that I provided certainly proved that the Esmond was in a patch of ice and it looked as though the Imogene was a very necessary part of the salvage since she was an icebreaker, and the resulting award was highly satisfactory to Bowring Brothers. The ice wasn't really very much to write home about and I can't really understand how the Esmond managed to lose her propeller in it. The two days spent with the Esmond made no difference to the seal fishery and the voyage to the ice commenced as planned on March 6th.

    The first thing to be done as we backed away from the wharf was to have the ship searched for stowaways. A small number were unearthed hiding in various spots that seemed to be well known to the crew and after they had been landed back on the dock, we set off for the Narrows and the Front. The ice field that year was as far south as St. John's but it was

Left: Sealing Capt. Al Blackwood whose son, David, became a well-known artist. Right: Lt. James Walwyn, R.N. pretending to do some work. Photos: *Derrick Bowring*

not, in fact, blocking the Narrows and we steamed through in good style. The Imogene was probably the last one through the Narrows but because of her ability to move in the ice field, over the course of the next two or three hours we managed to pass all other vessels on our way north. As we steamed north, more stowaways were unearthed from places that hadn't been thought of. I think two of them had buried themselves in the coal bunkers, but it was too late to land them and they completed the six-week trip with us. Aboard the Imogene as we started the voyage were the following: the sealing captain, Al Blackwood; the navigator, Capt. Eugene Burden, who was the only member of the crew with a Master's ticket and therefore required for the ship to clear customs; the chief engineer, William McGettigan; and also four engineers, 12 firemen, cooks, stewards, bakers and about 300 sealers. It was a very full load of people, plus the ship's bunkers and the holds filled with good Welsh coal necessary to keep her steaming through the ice for six to eight weeks. Added to that were six stowaways and two passengers: Lt. James Walwyn, R.N., son of the current governor of the island and on leave from the navy to act as his father's aide-de-camp, and myself as an interested spectator of all that was going on.

About to enter the ice – ship going slow ahead so as not to crash too heavily. *Photo: Derrick Bowring*

The sealing crew was organized under four masters of watch, known colloquially as master watches. Each had a deputy who was responsible for the four teams of men while on the ice and whose duty it was to bring them back to the ship at the end of the day's work. It was a vital job and their success in bringing everyone home in the evening never ceased to amaze me, for the four crews of sealers would be gone from the beginning of the day to its end and would be well away from the ship on the ice – so far from the ship that I couldn't even see them – but they always returned safely before dark. Needless to say, each master watch held a roll call of his men when they were back on board. Nobody was lost.

Then there were the barrelmen. There was always one man in the lower barrel on the foremast who was responsible for conning the ship through the ice fields. From the height of his barrel, he was better able to see the leads in the ice than anybody working from the lower level of the bridge. The barrel at the top of the foremast was used when we were seriously looking for seals because, from that vantage point, one could see a far greater distance than anyone

Men gearing up to go over the side.
Photo: Derrick Bowring

else; in addition, that barrel was equipped with one of the most enormous telescopes I had ever seen.

The man in the top barrel was the barrelman and the one in the lower was the "scunner," who gave directions to the bridge as to the course the helmsman should steer. On the bridge itself was the helmsman at the wheel in the wheelhouse, and a bridge master who was actually in charge of the directions given to the engine room whenever we were trying to butt our way through heavy ice. Mostly the Imogene could steam through ordinary ice and I recall that we were steaming at five knots through ice when other vessels close by us were jammed. She was a highly useful performer in the ice fields.

At this particular point the stowaways were a perfect nuisance for they would nip out onto the ice to grab a flipper or two and nobody in particular watched what they were up to but they had to be checked in again in the evening. They were a further bother because

Strapping on seals – note the roughness of the ice. *Photo: Derrick Bowring*

Every man bringing a tow at the end of a day's work. *Photo: Derrick Bowring*

they had to be fed as well. We had plenty of food on board for at least eight weeks and the ship's fresh water tanks were, of course, filled before leaving but were insufficient for the full voyage with that number of men on board. They were replenished from time to time by hauling "young icebergs" on board with the aid of the ship's winches; these were large pieces of ice that had broken off larger icebergs and which were, of course, fresh water. Once brought on board, they were broken up and shoved into the tanks where they rapidly melted, and no problem was encountered over a lack of water to drink or to cook with.

For the first 10 days of our voyage we searched the Atlantic Ocean from Cape Bonavista as far north as Battle Harbour and it was not until the 11th day, the 17th of March, that we actually found the main patch of seals and the Imogene "burnt down" in the patch for the night. We were in the latitude, or maybe a little farther north, of Battle Harbour, which is north of the Straits of Belle Isle and not very many miles off the coast. The noise the seals make in the patch, and there must have been thousands of them, was quite unbelievable and I had never seen such a sight or heard such a sound in my life. The next morning at the crack of dawn, the sealers were out, each armed with a gaff a little satchel of lunch and a tow rope. They always kept to their own watches under their master watch and they always worked in pairs. Nobody went off single-handed in a special direction of his own. He always had someone else with him for obvious safety reasons as, while the ice was thick enough to carry as many men as you like, the pans were sometimes in slack ice and had water slosh in them that looked like ice, but was not strong enough to carry a man's weight. Not that the experienced sealer ever did so, but it was possible to fall in. As the day progressed, the sealers on the ice were totally lost to view of anyone left onboard the ship. It was one of the real miracles to me how groups of men assembled in their appropriate watch could be seen in a long line of sealers heading towards the ship and each man had a tow of seals that he was bringing back on board. The bulk of the seals that had been taken that day had been collected on the largest pan of ice that could be found and marked with the Imogene's own flag. They were now ready to be picked up in the next day's activities as the ship steamed around the ocean pulling up beside the pan of ice with the seals on it. The most useful thing that James Walwyn and I did during the voyage was to relieve the helmsman during the day so that he could assist with strapping on seal pelts as we steamed around to pick them up. We also operated the winches to assist in the hauling aboard of the pelts. Occasionally, we were on the ice with a rope used for strapping on the seals and hooking onto the end of the winch, which had an extra length of wire hawser to enable the pans to be hauled in when still some distance from the ship. It kept us entertained and exercised and we certainly obtained plenty of fresh air.

Sealer with a tow headed to the SS Imogene.
Photo: Derrick Bowring

Seal pelts are, by nature, very slippery. On one side there is the hair or fur skin of the seal and on the other there is several inches of oily fat, which provides the slip. The pelts were hauled onboard from the pans on the ice where they had been collected together; a pan load was picked up as quickly as possible and, as they were brought on board, were simply dumped on the deck, either the foredeck or the afterdeck. This process continued while the ship moved around from one pan of seals to the next. It wasn't until after the sealing crews had come back on board in the evening that the pelts were finally stowed and counted or tallied in the hold. The hold itself had been prepared for this slippery and highly movable cargo by being divided into smaller sections known as pounds. Once pitched in a pound, the pelts could not move very far and this restriction prevented the cargo from heaving from side to side and possibly endangering the ship as the vessel rolled or pitched in the sea. The crew sent the pelts down the hatch into the pound that was being filled while a tallyman kept track of the numbers. A tally was a count of 10 pelts plus one but was counted as 10. The total count of pelts was reported to the St. John's office by radio each evening. The number of seals was totaled by the tallies counted up to 10 but one knew that there was always the extra seal to be found when the cargo was unloaded at the Southside. On one of the days when we had been picking up seals we had a real deck load of them and by the time we had worked our way to the outer edge of the ice field, the ocean swell was coming

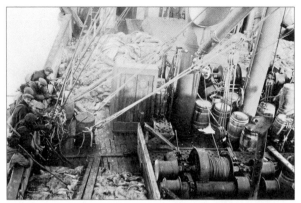
A load of pelts, and men going over the side again.
Photo: Derrick Bowring

in from the east and raising the pans quite severely. The deck cargo of loose pelts caused us to roll in a highly unpleasant fashion and I remember Captain Blackwood deciding that it was too uncomfortable for us to have our tea and so we steamed back into the ice to find calmer conditions that would suit our stomachs.

One of the things you really needed at the seal fishery during what was mostly fine sunny weather was a good pair of sunglasses, otherwise you would be snow blind – a serious condition. We were in the main patch for the best part of a week and the Imogene, because of her superior ability to move around in the ice, was in the patch for a full two days before any other vessels penetrated it even though they knew where the patch was. The picking up of the seals that had been panned in the main patch was completed in about 10 days and we then set off again looking for other patches or waiting until the next round could take place, when we would be after "bedlamers." Bedlamers are immature seals, either one or two years old, that keep together for some reason best known to themselves and are extremely skittish. They were not in very big patches and they had to be approached with great caution, for if they took fright, they'd all disappear into the water.

Towards the end of March, when we had picked up all the seals obtained from the main patch, we found ourselves searching for new patches of seals. We were at about the latitude of Battle Harbour heading towards the Strait of Belle Isle when we found ourselves in what is called a "running joint." This is where the ice, which normally moves continually as it is carried by the Arctic current, is travelling in a southerly direction but as it moves it occasionally encounters land, rocks, islands or even icebergs that have run aground. This obviously prevents the ice field from moving any further south. A running joint is where part of the ice field has been stopped and the ice adjoining that stopped part is still moving in a southerly direction carried by the current. Where the two join is the running joint and on this occasion the Imogene was part of the ice pack right in the joint. We were heading in a southerly direction and on our starboard side we were moving, but on our port side we were not moving through the ice. The reason for this anomaly was that the port side ice had been stopped by a gigantic iceberg several miles ahead that had run aground to the north of Cape Bald, the northernmost part of Newfoundland. The ice that was moving with us was clear of the iceberg and was heading eventually into the Strait of Belle Isle. The Imogene was part of the ice field and was unable to wiggle out to the right due to the pressure of the ice. The port side ice was as tight as it could possibly be since it was driven up against the immovable iceberg. We therefore moved at the speed of the ice flowing into the Strait, and as we moved slowly southward, passing the stopped ice on our port side and travelling with the same pan of ice on our starboard side, we were obviously going to come very close to the stationary iceberg. It was a somewhat unnerving moment, at least to the likes of me, who reckoned that icebergs might stick out in all directions under the water and the Imogene could well have some very serious damage done to her as we passed it. However, good fortune was with us and we literally slithered along the side of the iceberg – from the bridge you could almost lean out and touch the side of it. Time slowed as we passed, but finally shot out like a cork out of a bottle into what was virtually open water. This enabled us to move in whatever direction we liked and I, for one, felt highly relieved at the outcome.

Iceberg in the Strait of Belle Isle that we passed so close that you could almost touch it from the deck.
Photo: Derrick Bowring

We were then in the Strait of Belle Isle in relatively open water and able to move around quite freely. It became apparent that there were no seals to be found by proceeding further in this direction and, on top of that, a radio message was received from St. John's reporting that a patch of seals had been spotted by landsmen in the area of Groais Island. Captain Blackwood decided that he might as well turn around and head in that direction. We knew there was certainly plenty of ice on which seals might well be lodged so we turned around to head north again and go around the northern tip of the island. As we were heading out of the strait, a wireless message was received from the Ungava, one of Job Brothers' ships, which was also in the strait, asking whether the Imogene would be good enough to help her get out of the ice she was in since she had damaged her rudder and was in some degree of peril. My own thought was that the custom and laws of the sea would require that we go to her assistance, but Blackwood paid no attention whatsoever and kept the Imogene heading away from the Ungava, which was further into the strait than we had been. I asked him whether he intended to help the Ungava, to which he replied, "Not at all. There's absolutely nothing wrong with the Ungava. He can get out of there if he wants to. He's just trying to pull the wool over our eyes so we can give him a lift from where he's stuck. Silly bugger. We're going to Groais Island." And off we went. We then rounded Cape Norman and

Ships forcing through very heavy ice near Groais Island – Neptune, Beothic and Ungava astern of the Imogene. *Photo: Derrick Bowring*

Cape Bald and on the way around these capes, we passed Bowring's Terra Nova, which was having difficulty in fairly substantial ice through which the Imogene could steam at about five knots. Since the Terra Nova was a Bowring ship, the Imogene went over towards her and enabled the Terra Nova to get into the wake of the Imogene, thus providing broken and fairly loose ice through which she was able to steam freely on her own. In that form, we proceeded around the capes and headed south. In the process, another of Job's ships, the Neptune, also got herself into the Imogene's wake. The Neptune was a competent ship in ice so the procession was the Imogene followed by the Neptune, and then the Terra Nova. The ships following the Imogene always had loose and broken ice so they were able to maintain their speed without any difficulty.

The Imogene, for all her ability in the ice, occasionally came up against a substantial pan that had to be broken before she could proceed, and occasionally this meant going astern and taking a second run at it. The two ships behind her had to keep their wits about them or there would be general chaos around the Imogene's stern. On one occasion when the Imogene backed up to have another go at a large pan of ice, the crew of the Neptune, the ship immediately behind her, hadn't been paying attention and only managed to stop when the Neptune's bowsprit, which was long because she was an old-fashioned whaler, was hanging over the Imogene's stern. She did manage to avoid hitting the Imogene but there could have been substantial and irritating damage done to both ships. After that she maintained her distance in a more discreet way. The whole convoy traveled onwards the Grey Islands, in fact past Groais Island and Bell Island and into some pretty heavy ice to the south of the islands. We burnt down for the night, hoping to find some seals in the morning. All we found was a lot of northeasterly wind, heavy snow and generally hopeless conditions, and the ice

Jammed in the ice – men trying to force the ice around the stern in order to turn the ship. *Photo: Derrick Bowring*

Entering the Narrows in a slight haze at the end of the trip. *Photo: Derrick Bowring*

packed so tight that nobody could move, and there we stayed for three or four days of irritation and frustration. To finalize this incident, who should appear to join us south of the Grey Islands but the Ungava, obviously having discovered that there was nothing wrong with her rudder whatsoever. This request for aid was considered to be typical of her captain, Billy Winsor, who was known as a wily old character.

One day when the Imogene was stuck in the ice and we were waiting for a wind shift to free things up, we realized that there was a bobbing hole about a hundred yards off our position and Captain Blackwood thought it would be interesting for his two rather bored passengers to take a rifle each and squat beside the bobbing hole in the hope that a seal might pop up and with a quick shot we would have a seal. We thought that would be a pleasant little excursion. Captain Blackwood also had in mind that we were, in his view, pretty stupid on the ice and he sent one of his most reliable master watches to keep an eye on us while we sat by the hole. Well, we sat by the hole for at least two hours, perhaps more.

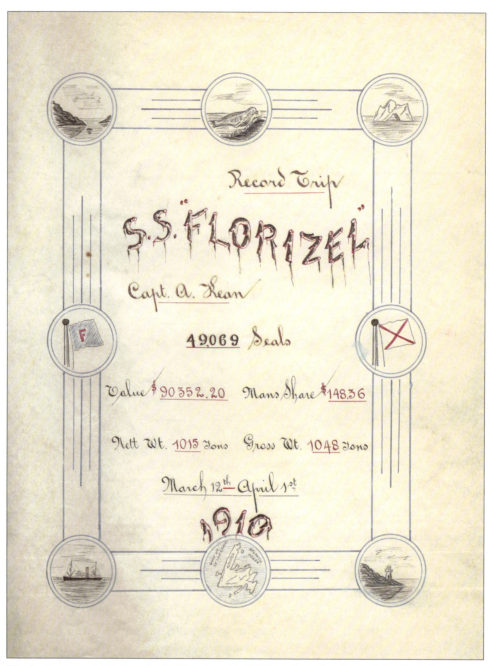

The front page of Eric Bowring's diary from his 1910 sealing trip aboard the Florizel – a historic trip.

Nothing whatever happened. We never got a shot at anything and all we got from the endeavour were rather numb extremities and so did our escort. We thought that the best way to reward him would be to offer him a glass of our supply of rum, which we fully intended to use ourselves. "Oh yes, I'd like that," he said, so we handed him a bottle of rum and a tumbler. He half filled the tumbler, handed the bottle back to one of us and poured it down his throat without benefit of anything to reduce its strength and then, with the reply of, "Thank you, that was very welcome," he departed back to his quarters. It was a quantity of rum that I would have used at least a bottle of something to reduce to more manageable levels. It was an impressive display.

I don't recall the number of pelts that we brought back through the Narrows but it would have been a goodly amount and I think we fared well against the competing vessels. My Uncle Eric had been on a record-setting sealing trip in 1910 when the SS Florizel brought back the largest number of seals ever caught in one trip to the ice. It was important to Bowring Brothers that upper management understood what the men endured during sealing expeditions, and I have to agree that it was an incredibly educational experience.

In August 1936, I made a trip in Bowring's SS Beothic to Tommy's Arm in Notre Dame Bay to load pulpwood for Barrow-in-Furness in England. This came about because one of the company's money-making activities was to arrange contracts with United Kingdom consumers of pulpwood or pit props and then subcontract the deal to a local merchant who had cutting rights on Crown land and was able to organize cutting the pulpwood, preparing it for export and loading it onto a chartered ship. In this case, the contract was for pulpwood for the Barrow Paper Mills Limited and the subcontractor in Newfoundland was a man called A.J. Hewlett, who operated in Notre Dame Bay and lived in Robert's Arm. The loading of the wood was to take place in Tommy's Arm, the next arm to the south, since that was the outlet of the river down which the pulpwood logs would be driven. Normally, Bowring's would have chartered a vessel to carry the pulpwood to England, but during the cutting season for the woods, which is in the winter, the transatlantic freight rates had risen to such an extremely high level that, if we had to pay out such a large sum to carry the wood to England, it would be better to use one of our own ships. Hence the Beothic. Although it was usually used as a seal fishery vessel, it was actually built in 1918 as an American Liberty ship of the First World War and was really a cargo vessel strengthened to go in the ice. My part in this activity was to act as supercargo, that is to attend to the preparation of the bill of lading after the cargo had been loaded and the total quantity known, to prepare the customs form for U.K. importation, and give the necessary information about the value of the cargo to St. John's for insurance purposes.

Top Left: Approaching Tommy's Arm aboard the SS Beothic. Top Middle: Loading pontoons coming alongside the Beothic. Centre: Wood floated down to Beothic so loading can begin. Top Right: Men at work on pontoons. Middle Left: No. 3 hatch almost full. Middle Right: SS Beothic showing deckload fore and aft. Bottom Left: Deckload nearing completion. Bottom Right: SS Beothic sails for Barrow-in-Furness, England. *Photos: Derrick Bowring*

The loading of the pulpwood took quite a time for it was done almost log by log. The Beothic had four hatches, two fore and two aft, and when we had anchored in the right position for loading, four rafts, which had been specially constructed, were floated alongside the vessel opposite each of the hatches. The raft was built so that two men could stand on a separate platform on either side of the raft where the middle was open and into which logs could be floated and pushed into position. Before the logs came in, a strap was put across from one platform to the other so that when the space was full of logs and carefully measured to produce exactly one cord of wood, 128 cubic feet, the strap ends could be brought together. Then the hook from the winch on deck was attached and the whole cord was hoisted up and lowered into the appropriate hold onboard the Beothic where the logs were stowed cord by cord until the hold was filled.

This went on at each of the four hatches. It took a considerable time, as one can imagine, and there was a large crew of men on the raft pushing logs toward it and stowing them once the load reached the hold. When the holds were filled to the brim, more cargo was stowed on deck to a considerable height because, being wood, it was not a deadweight cargo, and the vessel, even filled up to her hatches, was by no means down to her marks. The cargo on deck was piled high and upright stanchions were attached to the rails of the vessel with the whole thing lashed down in what was intended to get the full load across the Atlantic. During the crossing, some of the deck cargo was lost because of rough weather, but as she sailed away from Tommy's Arm, she made quite a sight looking like a floating lump of wood with a funnel and two masts.

The plan was that when all was loaded and accounted for, the Beothic would sail for Barrow-in-Furness, calling in at Twillingate, which was the nearest port from which she could "clear" customs for the high seas and where I would be deposited to make my own way back to St. John's by coastal boat. However, I did not return that way as the evening before the departure of the Beothic, we had a visit from the SS Argyle, one of the old Reid Coastal Boats then run by the Newfoundland Railway and at that time chartered to Bowater's Paper Company of the U.K. They were considering buying the International Paper Company Mills in Corner Brook. A small party of Bowater people were on board touring the coast and assessing wood availability. The Argyle's captain was Wes Kean, an old Bowring captain who, having cleared the matter with the senior Bowater man on board, volunteered to take me with them to St. John's, which they would reach in two or three days' time. So I had a pleasant cruise on what was essentially a private yacht, only to arrive in St. John's to receive a rocket for not having told them the value of the cargo for insurance purposes. The only way I could contact St. John's from Tommy's Arm was by the telegraph system operated by the Post Office. Nobody lived at Tommy's Arm so I had written out the necessary telegram and asked the foreman of the loading crew to send it from Robert's Arm, where they all lived, and to which they returned each evening. Apparently, he forgot to send it.

There were two events on this trip that have always remained in my memory. The first one had to do with the fact that we must all have eaten something that we should not have for one night we were all stricken with a dose of "summer complaint" which caused a bit of commotion because while the Beothic was adequately supplied with toilets, they were hardly sufficient to cope with this sudden influx and there were some extraordinary queues outside the doors of these facilities one night and early morning. However, we all recovered quickly except for the first mate, who was an elderly man and took several days to get back to normal. I was very sorry for him.

The other event was considerably more fun and involved an expedition by the captain of the Beothic, Eugene Burden, and the chief engineer, both of whom had little to do while the loading of the pulpwood was going on, and certainly I had nothing to do but enjoy myself. We took one of the ship's dories to go on a fishing trip up the river down which the logs had been driven to Crescent Lake, which was some way up, and try our hand at getting a few trout. One of the loading crew told us that we should keep an eye open as there was certainly one bear, if not more, around Crescent Lake and the captain therefore decided that he would take his ship's revolver with him – not so much to shoot the bear but at least to frighten it. It all seemed perfectly normal to me and off we went in our dory. We weren't going to take the dory up the river so we rowed ashore as far up as we could reasonably go and anchored the dory with the grapnel it had on board embedded in the sands and the rocks of the beach. Then we walked our way up the riverbank until we came to Crescent Lake where we set about on our extraordinarily unsuccessful fishing venture. I think we only managed to find one poor benighted trout. Regardless, we had a pleasant day and then worked our way back down the river to row ourselves out to the Beothic. However, when we got back to where we had left the dory, we found the tide had risen quite considerably and the dory was a good many yards offshore still attached to its grapnel. There was only one thing to be done and that was to swim out to the dory. At this point of course, Burden still had his revolver in his hip pocket somewhere and I said to him, "What are you going to do with the revolver? You'll ruin it if you swim out with that in your pocket." He said, "Oh no, I'll fix that." He was wearing his captain's hat so he took the hat off, turned it upside down, put the revolver in the hat, balanced the whole thing on his head and took to the water. The three of us then swam out to the dory, clambered aboard, the hat and the revolver still in place on the captain's head.

As I look back on these various trips and excursions, such as the seal fishery, the tour on the railway line, the pulpwood loading and other smaller expeditions to various places, I realize how brilliant my decision was to accept a job in Newfoundland with Bowring Brothers instead of looking for one in England that would probably involve being stuck in an office all day and every day, and traipsing up and back from it by railway, which my father did for many years. I had escaped that and substituted something for it that was a lot more fun, a lot more interesting and had a lot more variety. Lucky me! Added to that, I had landed amongst the most wonderful people who had a glorious sense of how life should be lived, a great sense of humour, kindness beyond belief and a real joy in living and laughing. These expeditions through the bays and inlets of the east coast were my introduction to waters that, ever since, have given me untold pleasure, sailing on them, and meeting with and enjoying their wonderful people. In fact, I eventually bought a house in Burnside, Bonavista Bay.

Newfoundlanders also have a most wonderful and picturesque way of describing things, especially my tutor, Walter Wills, who really was a past master at describing something in a way that made it quite clear to you what he was on about. He had one unforgettable description of somebody we were discussing whose name he mentioned but didn't ring a bell with me at first; I was looking puzzled and trying to think who the man was when Walter said, "You know him, that broken-assed bugger," meaning a man who, sadly for him, had some hip deformity and walked with difficulty and a considerable limp, but with Walter's description, I realized who he was talking about immediately. Since Walter Wills had lived his entire life in St. John's, and was in his 70s when I met him, he knew every nook and corner of the city and knew it by its familiar and historical colloquial names such as Maggoty Cove and the Barking Kettle and so on, and obviously over the years, in conversation with him, I

Our house in Burnside, which also became a retreat for much of the family over the decades.

absorbed a great deal of this local knowledge. Many years later, probably in the 1970s, I was playing a game of Trivial Pursuit, the Newfoundland version, with my wife, my sister-in-law and one or two other Newfoundlanders who had grown up in the province from their infancy. I could beat them quite easily, much to their astonishment. "How on earth do you know all these things when you weren't even here as a boy?" Of course the answer was that I had the world's finest tutor in Newfoundland folklore in the shape of Walter Woodman Wills.

CHAPTER FOUR
"GIG" BAIRD

When I arrived in 1935, St. John's was a relatively small city where, as they say, everybody knew everybody. Not strictly true but I certainly landed in a section of the community that had an organized and entertaining life of its own. There were many around my own age and quite a few, both male and female, had been in England for part or most of their education. Up to the time of Confederation, the United Kingdom was home. After all, that was where most of the population had originated over the centuries. The Furness Withy boat was the home boat.

Our amusements were simple and inexpensive. None of us had any money. We were still in the Depression even if slowly emerging from it. We had the movies – there were at least three separate movie houses in St. John's, the most expensive one cost 35 cents and the other two were 25 cents. We had private parties and some public dances to raise money for, in many cases, schools or churches. We had a golf course plus skiing, skating, trout and salmon fishing, partridge shooting, swimming in ponds as the sea was too cold, and there was one privately owned squash court. In the basement of the Bishop Feild College, there was a 25-yard miniature shooting range.

In February 1936, I was invited to a party at a private house on Circular Road where they were holding a dance for a niece who was visiting from England. The house belonged to Avalon and Nita Goodridge. I duly turned up and went through the motions of joining in the dancing until we came to a dance that in my day was known as a Paul Jones. A Paul Jones was designed to mix the guests up a bit and it consisted of the men joining hands in a large circle facing inwards and the girls forming their circle inside the boys' circle while facing outwards. When the music started, the girls' circle moved in a clockwise direction and the boys revolved counterclockwise. When the music stopped, the person who was standing opposite you became your partner for the next leg of the dance. By this time I had come to know quite a number of people in St. John's society, but not all of them. In one round of the Paul Jones, the music stopped and there standing opposite me was Moira Gordon Baird. I had finally met that lovely, laughing, joyous girl, quick of wit and word, who was later to become my beloved wife and devoted friend for 50 happy years. It was a moment for the history book but history demanded that I do a bit of work before things were sorted out.

The first problem was that she had a boyfriend but that turned out to be not too big a difficulty since she was quite a strong-minded Presbyterian and her boyfriend was a Roman Catholic. I did not know either of these facts at the time and he seemed to be an obstacle that somehow had to be removed. The other problem was that when one of my friends later said to her, "Derrick Bowring is keen on you," her reply was, "Look, Douglas, I'm not cradle-snatching!" Over time we became friends, then we became good friends and finally, after I had passed that milestone of my 21st birthday, which in those days was when you theoretically became an adult, I popped the question and thank God, she said "Yes"! Some years later, I remember asking her, "When was it that you decided that you would say yes if I asked you to marry me?" Her answer, I was surprised to hear, was, "I decided when you were out at the seal fishery," so at least it proves that absence does make the heart grow fonder. The result was entirely satisfactory, certainly to me and I believe to her and our resulting family.

Moira Gordon "Gig" Baird, c. 1936.

Her father, David M. Baird, died in 1932 as the result of a heart attack. He had been a manufacturer's representative and was the agent for companies such as Johnson & Johnson and Proctor & Gamble when they were still relatively small organizations. He had a team of salesmen who travelled the province getting these various products into little shops and he did very well at it; in fact, he was the first person in Newfoundland to buy a Chrysler car, which cost about $500 at the time. He also had a reputation for kindness. He once saw a man beating a horse to motivate it into getting up a hill so he bought the horse and retired it to a friend's farm where it could live out its days in a meadow. His children were Frances (Frank) born in 1912, Moira Gordon (Gig) born 1916, and David Monroe (Mun) born in 1921.

Gig's mother, Em, had been born Emma Ash, the youngest daughter of a redoubtable seaman, Captain Francis Ash, of Trinity. Every earlier

David Baird, c. 1922.

Captain Francis Ash (centre) aboard the SS Bear, 1884.

Emma Baird, c. 1963.

generation of the Ash family had been a seaman and Gig's grandfather had been captain of the ship Portia, a passenger and cargo vessel owned by Bowring's Red Cross Line, which ran from St. John's to Halifax and on to New York. He had even participated in an Arctic search-and-rescue mission for Lt. Adolphus Greely who had led an ill-fated, and later infamous, U.S. Army science expedition in the 1880s. The U.S. Navy–led Greely Relief had commissioned the SS Bear out of Trinity and Captain Ash and a small crew took her down to New York for the navy's use. Some pre-mission socializing led to the realization that Captain Ash had valuable experience navigating a ship through ice and, consequently, he was given a temporary commission by the U.S. Navy as the ice pilot for the Greely Relief. The family story was that he had telegraphed his wife that night to ask her if she would mind his going on this expedition to which she replied, "Would it matter?" And that was that – off he went.

Emma Baird was kindness itself to me when I first started appearing at her house. None of us had any money to spare and whenever Gig and I went off to a movie (25 cents at the Star and Nickel and 35 cents at the Capital), she would tell us to be sure to come back to her house after, remarking, "Derrick cannot afford to be buying coffee and cookies at the Blue Puttee," a local snack bar. So we used to adjourn to 24 Monkstown Rd, to the upstairs sitting room, where there was always a cup of tea and cake or cookies. On some much later occasion, when Gig and I were having an argument, I said, "Well, your mother agrees with me." The reply was, "Oh, Mother always agrees with you." I ventured to ask why she should do that, only to be told, "Oh, just because you're a Bowring, that's why!"

Mrs. Baird was an expert at burning the bottom out of kettles. She used to boil the kettle for the tea on a gas ring that was situated in the bathroom of their house on the second floor, which was where the sitting room was, too. She was one of the best customers of Bowring's hardware department, being a constant buyer of new kettles. Finally she thought she had the problem licked when she found she could buy a kettle that was equipped with a whistle, which went off when the steam started to emerge from the boiling kettle. I discovered, fairly soon after she acquired it, that I could imitate the whistle of the kettle by doing it through my teeth and when I knew she had put the kettle on in the bathroom, I gave it a little time while she settled back in her chair, and then produced the whistling sound, which sent her off to the bathroom only to come back saying, "That kettle wasn't boiling ... I'm sure I heard the whistle." Eventually the penny dropped and she caught me at it, which produced a few threatening noises but which was all taken with good humour, because, of all things, she had a great sense of humour.

Much later, when I had asked Gig to marry me and she had agreed, I went off to ask for her mother's permission. I did so in the same sitting room upstairs and Gig was told to keep out of the way so her mother and I were closeted in the sitting room. I asked Em if I might marry her daughter and she said yes and we then went on to discuss various interesting things about Trinity, about various ships and other fascinating matters. We had long moved on from the topic of our initial chat and had managed to forget that the subject of said chat was growing ever more impatient in the hall. Eventually, Gig could stand it no longer and she barged into the sitting room saying, "Surely Mother has answered your question by now!" Neither her mother nor I was ever allowed to forget that lapse. To put it plainly, no man ever had a better mother-in-law than I did. She really was a gem and I always enjoyed her company and her opinions, which were very sound and to the point. I think the most marvellous remark she ever made on my behalf came at a ladies tea party in the spring of 1939, when it was known that I was to be one of the honorary aides-de-camp (ADC) at Government House on the occasion of the visit of King George VI and Queen Elizabeth. One of the ladies made the unfortunate remark that it was a bit surprising that I should have been picked as one of the six since my mother was of German extraction, although born in England and, in fact, always a British subject. Em Baird's reply to this comment was that, "Well, I think that King George's mother is also of German extraction." That flattened the lady who ventured to make the comment. I never was able to find out who she actually was.

In December 1937, I made my first trip back to England to be there in time for Christmas and the New Year and didn't return to Newfoundland until March of 1938. While we were crossing the Atlantic on the westbound trip, Hitler invaded Austria and the Anschluss took place. Not very good news to anybody, I'm afraid. Later that year, my brother Norman, who had just left Shrewsbury School to start a career, joined the Territorial Army in England. The foreshadowings of war were commencing.

In the summer of 1938, my parents and brother and sister came out for a holiday visit to St. John's. They participated in all the local activities, sailing in Placentia Bay on my uncle's schooner, all the local parties, of which there were plenty, and generally became acclimatized to life out here. They also met Gig, which set their minds at rest because they didn't really know what it was I had got myself hitched to.

In the spring of 1939, I made a trip on the Red Cross line, St. John's to Halifax to New York, where I spent about 10 days under the aegis of Bowring and Company familiarizing myself with what they did for Bowring Brothers as our American agents, a function they had fulfilled for many years. I came back to St. John's on the return trip of the same vessel and found that one of my fellow passengers, an American called Walter Wehner, who was roughly my contemporary, was representing the American Radiator and Standard Sanitary Company of the U.S. whose products Bowring Brothers sold in St. John's. He was a congenial young man and Gig was able to take him in charge when, a few days later, I had to perform at Government House as an ADC to the Governor, who had a huge influx of dignitaries and admirals and Lord knows what for a lunch, a garden party and for generally looking after the King and Queen and their entourage.

This activity took me out of action as far as anyone else was concerned so Gig took Walter down to a vantage point on the roof of a house near the War Memorial at which the King was due to lay a wreath. Walter Wehner took it all in, took many photographs and, as he watched the proceedings, got very emotional. It really was quite moving because there was an Honour Guard of Great War veterans drawn up at the Memorial. The King and Queen went down the ranks chatting to many of the men and finally, the wreath was laid with Newfoundland's Governor – Vice-Admiral Humphrey Walwyn – and several admirals in attendance. By that point, Walter Wehner was moved to tears and exclaimed, "Why don't we have a King?"

One of the more entertaining moments arose at Government House just after they had finished the official lunch for the King and Queen and assorted visiting admirals. The King, who had been a naval officer in his own career and knew these admirals personally, took the senior one, who was the admiral commanding the West Indies Squadron, off to the Governor's study and the two of them sat down to have a cigarette and a chat. In fact, from where we ADCs were standing, we could see right down the passage into the study and there they were relaxing and enjoying themselves. Meanwhile the Governor, also a vice-admiral but not in on this private chat, was stomping up and down the hallway wondering how he was going to root the King out of the study because he had to get him pointed in the direction of his next appointment. We all found this quite entertaining because the Governor was not inclined to do things that didn't suit his own convenience. Meanwhile, the Queen was out in the hallway chatting to us whipper-snappers, which was certainly of interest to us and something that I have never forgotten. We suddenly realized that whether you are a King or a Queen, you're still just a human being.

Then came that appalling period in our lives – the Second World War – from September 1939 to May 1945, and August 1945 in the case of Japan. Nothing was ever the same again. Of course I had to join in but the first question was how was I going to do it? Newfoundland itself became involved in the war from the minute it was declared in London on September 3rd. However, Newfoundland had no military organization of any kind although a number of Newfoundlanders had, in the few months before the war, enlisted in the Royal Navy, especially when a Royal Navy ship appeared in St. John's. There were always half a dozen or more who joined by going aboard. The first thing that was asked for by the U.K. was Naval Volunteers and the number required was soon filled. I suppose most of my contemporaries felt that they really belonged in the Army and they knew nothing about the sea or the Navy. Being a member of the Territorial Army, my brother had been called up in England some weeks before the war was actually declared. It was not until February 1940 that it was announced that Newfoundland would be asked to form two heavy regiments of artillery as part of the British Army. The first objective was to enlist 900 men for the first regiment of which the first 400 would leave relatively quickly for training in the U.K. to be followed by the rest of the regiment and the second regiment to follow in its turn.

The first 400 were quickly enlisted and enjoyed some preliminary training, at least in marching and looking like soldiers though dressed as civilians, in the Church Lads' Brigade Armoury in St. John's. While all this martial behaviour took place, Gig and I announced our official engagement on Christmas Day 1939; we then discovered that the Army would only take single men between certain ages. Therefore, we had to somehow circumvent this quite ridiculous rule and we decided that the best thing would be for me to enlist, go overseas, get myself established in the regiment in the U.K. training to be a gunner, and Gig would obtain passage sometime in the summer on one of the paper boats that ran regularly from Newfoundland to the U.K. We would be able to get married over there. Such is the optimism of youth and we did achieve it, but not without considerable commotion in the process.

I left on April 14, 1940 with the first 400 packed into two trains heading for Port aux Basques. This took us a full 24 hours with engine-changing stops and a delay of some con-

My artillery unit. I'm the first from the left, kneeling, Woolwich Barracks, 1940.

siderable period in Grand Falls where we were greeted by the local population and given messages of good cheer to send us on our way. They were also busy recruiting men to come in second and third drafts later in the year. From Port aux Basques we went on two of the coastal boats, the Caribou and I think the Kyle, to Sydney, Nova Scotia, where we boarded a Canadian National train that took us to Saint John, New Brunswick. Our next mode of transport was the Canadian Pacific liner Duchess of Richmond, which was no longer a transatlantic liner but had become a troop ship. There were Canadian troops on board as well who were properly equipped with uniforms whereas we were dressed as civilians because we were to be outfitted when we reached the U.K. This led to a bit of a squabble as to what sort of idiots we were going to war looking like that, but it was settled amicably. After a day or so on board in Saint John, we then sailed and, to our surprise, arrived in Halifax where, I presume, we refuelled and then hung around until someone decided we could sail. We sailed on our own, without convoy but in the company of a rather old-fashioned Royal Navy cruiser, which I believe was called HMS Emerald. It was simply returning to the U.K. and chose to go with us. Halfway across the Atlantic, we met a Swedish merchantman heading west and at that time the Royal Navy was rounding up all neutral vessels and checking them out because they were suspected of being German vessels flying a neutral flag. HMS Emerald went after this particular vessel and we never saw her again. In due course, we arrived in Liverpool and were landed at what is known as the Prince's Landing and transferred immediately from ship to train for the run south; we didn't know where we were headed but it turned out to be Woolwich Barracks on the eastern outskirts of London, not far from the Greenwich Observatory.

Here we were issued uniforms and indulged in what was just parade ground drill so that we began to look like something that belonged to an army. There was also a certain amount of interviewing of individuals to see what they were capable of doing or what training they had in various activities of civilian life. At some time in May, I found myself shipped up to the 11th Field Training Regiment at Kimmel Park in North Wales where we moved into quite comfortable barracks that had been recently built for conscription in the U.K. before the war started. There I discovered I was to learn the mathematics of artillery firing, which essentially consists of trigonometry – something I hadn't touched for five or six years. At Kimmel Park, we had good sleeping quarters, a pleasant lecture room and not too strenuous activity on the parade ground with a 25-pounder gun. This comfortable life came to an end with the Dunkirk evacuation, which ended on June 4. The 300,000 plus troops, mostly without any equipment, had to then pile into any available barracks in the United Kingdom in order to try and sort them out and get them back into their designated units. We lost our sleeping quarters, our lecture room became where we slept and, on top of that, we lost our second battle dress, because these returning men had to be outfitted again and the quartermaster's stores simply didn't have enough uniforms. It was a total fiasco. Towards the latter part of June, we returned to the Newfoundland Regiment, which had its headquarters at Norwich, in the county of Norfolk. I found myself attached to D Battery, which had been divided into two half-batteries and the half to which I was joined was up in the woods near a little village called Little Walsingham of quite ancient, historical lineage. There, we installed two old six-inch naval guns that had been mounted on great iron wheels – totally unmanageable by the small crew we had – and we set about defending the east coast of England against German invasion. To illustrate how hard up the place was for equipment, which of course had all been lost in France, the ammunition for our guns was delivered in the local grocer's delivery van. I don't know where it came from.

While all this activity was going on, Gig, in St. John's, was being pressured by her relations, who kept saying, "Well, you won't go over now, will you? It's much too unsafe." Finally, she thought that she had better consult her own mother. The reply she received was, "Well, if it was your father that was over in England and I was here, I would go." No wonder I always thought I had the world's best mother-in-law. To encourage her, Em organized Gig's passage on the Anglo-Newfoundland Development (AND) Company paper carrier the Geraldine Mary, and in due course she set sail from Botwood on the northeast coast of Newfoundland for the United Kingdom.

When she arrived to board the Geraldine Mary, her name had been placed on the passenger list as Gordon Baird; consequently, she had been designated to share a room with Mr. Harry Craufuird Thomson, a retired barrister then in his 80s. Of course, this would not do and the crewman offered to move Mr. Thomson but Gig knew him and knew his age and insisted that she would happily move to new quarters rather than disturb Mr. Thomson. It was an offer that would save her life.

The Geraldine Mary joined a huge eastbound convoy approaching a hundred ships which, because of the scarcity of destroyers, corvettes and suitable escort vessels, had very few escorts. At a point about 300 miles west of the north coast of Ireland, at seven o'clock in the morning, 15 days after their the departure, the Geraldine Mary was torpedoed. When the explosion occurred only three were killed – two crewmen and Mr. Thomson. Thank God Gig had moved.

A ship that has a cargo of newsprint does not sink very quickly and, therefore, she and the crew had plenty of time to launch and board the lifeboats and pull away from the sinking ship. The weather, fortunately, was not too bad for the North Atlantic. Two lifeboat loads of the few passengers and the crew, and one life raft with the captain and chief engineer and one or two others pulled away from the ship. One lifeboat hoisted its sails and set off for Ireland. The second one, in which Gig was sitting with the other passengers, had the bosun of the Geraldine Mary in charge and he had been torpedoed at least once or twice before in the earlier 1914–1918 war. He instructed his lifeboat crew that they were not going to go anywhere. If they stayed where they were, the escorts knew where the Geraldine Mary had been hit and in due course somebody would be sent back to pick them up. So the life raft and this one lifeboat tied themselves together

Geraldine Mary sinking, August 4, 1940.

and used their oars and paddles to keep the lifeboat headed into the wind and sat there to await rescue. Eventually a Sunderland Flying Boat, which was flying quite low, was seen approaching and it, in turn, spotted them in the lifeboat and made a large circle around them; a window opened in the cockpit and somebody waved to them, which was reassuring as they then realized that they had genuinely been spotted. Later in the day a sloop, HMS Sandwich, appeared and picked up the contents of the lifeboat and the life raft and they were told to keep their lifejackets on because, while the Geraldine Mary had taken many hours to sink, the sloop, if hit, would go down in three minutes. How true that was, I don't really know.

One of the passengers, Gerald Harvey, was an engineer with the AND Company and was on his way to England to see how he could assist with the war effort. Although not old, he was certainly well over middle age. An aunt of his who lived in St. John's was renowned for giving people sailing to England a package of some kind or another to take over to her daughter Dorothy, who lived in England. Poor old Gerald had been given a package from his aunt that turned out to be a sponge cake. Since a sponge cake wasn't going to make it across the Atlantic in any condition fit to eat, he opened it up and he and the other passengers enjoyed the cake. When Gerald and the three women passengers were all in the same lifeboat, he said to them, "Well girls, I think we'll tell Aunt Ethel that the cake went down with the ship!"

HMS Sandwich then took the rescued party around the north of Scotland and eventually arrived at a little port called Methil on the north shore of the Firth of Forth. Here the rescued passengers and crew of the Geraldine Mary were landed and organized to proceed to whatever destination they had had in mind. One of the passengers was Jean Warren, wife of Gordon Warren, a member of the Regiment who they knew was stationed with me at Kimmel Park in North Wales. Gig and Jean had decided that when they landed, they would head for the nearest town to Kimmel Park, which was Ryll, and get themselves established in some boarding house, hotel or whatever might be available. They were, of course, treated as distressed British seamen and given such clothing from the mission to seamen as could be found to fit them, which of course wasn't much good to Gig. They thought they were well enough clothed to carry on a little further and were taken by bus to the Edinburgh railway station. There they made inquiries about how they could reach North Wales, which is not an easy trip, even in peacetime, and virtually unheard of in wartime. By this point, my father had discovered that the Geraldine Mary had been lost but that she and her passengers and all but two of her crew and one elderly passenger had been rescued. He had somehow discovered that Gig was heading for Edinburgh Station and finally, after a great deal of difficulty, he got through on the telephone to the station master in Edinburgh and asked if somebody could find a Miss Baird, who was an intended passenger going he knew not where. Luckily, she was found and went to the telephone in the station master's office to find her future father-in-law asking if she was all right and where was she planning to go. When she said North Wales, he immediately said, "Well don't go because Derrick is no longer there. Get on the train for London and we'll meet you at King's Cross Station." She boarded the next available train for London, which was jammed to the hatches, and found a seat sitting next to an Army sergeant who had equipped himself with a bottle of rum that he was quite prepared to share with her and other passengers. They made an eight-hour overnight journey, jammed like sardines, the train stopping every time it sensed there seemed to be an air raid underway. Air raids were not very frequent at that time, but there were spasmodic one-plane excursions that were more of a nuisance as a rule.

Finally they reached the London terminus where both my parents had come in the car equipped to meet, I don't know what they thought, a complete invalid … or somebody who was going to be in pretty bad shape because they were equipped with hot water bottles, hot coffee in Thermoses, blankets, rugs and pillows and Lord knows what else. To their astonishment, their future daughter-in-law came traipsing down the platform with apparently not a feather out of her and, although looking a bit tired, she certainly was very pleased to see them. While all these exciting and alarming events were going on, I, either in North Wales or sitting in the woods in Norfolk, knew nothing of what was happening and it was difficult to keep in touch with anybody. However, it was possible occasionally to get away from the gun position and into the local village, which was about half a mile away, and there find a telephone to contact my parents and find out what was going on in the family. I did this one evening early in August and my mother answered the phone and I asked if there was any news of Gig and she said, "Oh, yes dear, she's here. Would you like to speak to her? She's been torpedoed."

I suppose I was fairly speechless when, after a short interval, the voice I wanted to hear appeared over the telephone line and I must admit, she sounded just the same as ever, in good spirits and demanding to know when I could get a bit of leave to come down so that we could be married. That was in the early days of August 1940, and it was still possible to get seven days' leave. Most of the Newfoundlanders were using it to go up to London to see the sights and enjoy themselves. I applied for what was known as Compassionate Leave and obtained it fairly easily because in the Regiment, a Newfoundlander didn't mind if he had leave this week or next week or the week after, as long as he got it, and I believe somebody volunteered to change his leave for me to go right away and he would go the following week. I set off for the south and duly arrived in Merstham and turned up at the house where I found everybody in good form, including Gig, who seemed to be as bright and cheerful and as lovely looking as ever.

My parents and sister, Sonia, were all trying to plan how we could be married and get everything done within my seven-day leave. The biggest problem was that Gig had virtually no clothes. She arrived in what she stood up in and since then had borrowed various items from Sonia but they were not exactly the same size so clothes had to be bought for her. The service in the church had to be arranged, but this caused a problem as there would be no time for the banns to be called and a special licence would have to be issued. Plus there was the question of a wedding ring, and also potential guests who could be invited and still be able to arrive at very short notice. I had arrived at the Georgian House, my family home, on the Monday and by that time it was well on in the afternoon. Tuesday was spent with everybody rushing off in various directions to achieve the basic minimum of things in order to be ready for the wedding on Wednesday. Gig and I went up to London on the train and there she managed to acquire some very attractive and suitable garments for the wedding and afterwards, because she had absolutely nothing left of her trousseau. One of the problems was shoes, as English women apparently only have wide feet and Gig needed a narrow fitting. She eventually found them in a store that specialized in, as they called it, American sizes. My father, who was going up to work in London anyway, took some time out to visit the Bishop of Southwark to see about a special licence. The Bishop and his staff were well aware that there was a war on and that leaves came suddenly and didn't last very long, so there was no trouble about granting the special licence. In the evening, I paid a visit to the local Rector to sort out the question of the church itself and found that he had to be away; however, the parish curate would be glad to conduct the ceremony for us at two o'clock on Wednesday the 15th.

During the day, my mother phoned a number of friends and relations, mostly relations, who lived within reasonable distance of Merstham and who might be able to attend the wedding at such extremely short notice. She managed to round up a good selection of cousins and aunts and so forth whom I had known all my life and was glad to see at the wedding. Poor Gig was a bit isolated because she had hoped that her cousin, Stewart Ayre, who was with me in the army, would be able to attend the wedding and give her away. Under the circumstances it was impossible for him to get leave. My brother, who was my best man, could only manage to get the day off. He was not far from Merstham and arrived in the morning of the day of the wedding but departed as soon as the bride and groom left for the honeymoon. In the morning of the wedding day, my father, Gig and I went over to Reigate to do a few errands. He acquired a case of champagne and also bought the last iced wedding cake apparently made during the war. I would say it had to have been made before the war as when we came to cut it, you really needed something more like an axe than a knife to get through the icing. While he was getting the champagne and the cake, we went to the local jeweller to buy a wedding ring. Unfortunately, the only one that would fit her finger was an extremely thin band of gold and I really was a bit ashamed of it. Nevertheless that's what we had to use and she, of course, wore it for the rest of her life.

When Gig's cousin couldn't get leave to give her away, she decided that the fallback person should be Lionel Cole, the brother of her brother-in-law Harvey Cole, who lived fairly close and whom she knew but hadn't seen for years. He was phoned and was willing to appear and so he and his wife, whom none of us knew or had ever set eyes on, appeared at the front door of the Georgian House and announced to a blank stranger that he had come to give the bride away. Anyway, he did the job in good form and I think enjoyed the party.

A couple of members of the regiment who had got wind of the wedding plans managed to turn up as guests, Jimmy Winter and George Martin. Also my two cousins Joan and Pix Bowring, who were both married by then, and their mother were there, as well as some others whom Gig knew, but most of the guests were blank strangers to her. However, she soon became acquainted with them and the reception at the Georgian House was a very successful affair since it was a beautiful day and the sun was shining.

The Battle of Britain was raging overhead and one could see the contrails of the aircraft weaving around in the sky. This rather alarmed one of the guests who was a naval officer normally stationed at Chatham where he worked in the naval hospital as a doctor – Chatham used to be bombed on a fairly regular basis. So when aeroplanes were in the sky overhead he was accustomed to taking shelter and certainly wouldn't be waltzing around on the lawn at the back of the house without any precautions. He suggested that we ought to be indoors but was overruled by everybody else.

For our honeymoon I had booked a room at the White Hart Hotel in Dorking about 10 miles away from Merstham and within range of where my father's car could reasonably travel.

Gig and I on our wedding day, August 15th, 1940.

We were, of course, limited as to how far we could travel because of gasoline rationing. Father drove us over to Dorking, under a shower of rose petals from the garden, and we got to the hotel safely. He came in for a drink and later departed and we were on our own. We had dinner that evening and in due course retired to our room when the air-raid sirens went off. We were blacked out in the hotel and even though we had a light on in the bedroom, it couldn't be seen outside and, as was the custom at the Georgian House, we paid no attention to the siren. However, that didn't suit the hotel in Dorking and hotel staff came around banging on the guests' doors and telling them to come and shelter in the basement in what they considered to be an air-raid shelter.

The White Hart Hotel was an extremely old building, I mean centuries old, and originally had been part of a monastery. The basement and cellars and underground works at the hotel had originally been the monks' wine cellar and were really quite extensive. I don't think it would have been much of a shelter but might save you from flying bricks, I suppose. We were driven down into the hotel basement with other guests, the odd dog and the hotel staff and there we stayed on our wedding night until the all clear sounded and we were allowed back upstairs to our rooms and bed. What a great wedding night that was.

This happened on the Wednesday night, the Thursday night and Friday night and by that time we'd had enough of being chivvied down into this wretched basement. At the Georgian House, while the air-raid warning sirens sounded quite frequently, they very often didn't really signify that there was going to be any enemy action and although occasionally a German plane would fly over, you could always tell them apart because they had a different sound to the RAF planes. In Merstham the family ignored them unless something actually dropped pretty close. After some discussion we decided that really, honeymoon or no honeymoon, we would be far better off at the Georgian House, where we would at least get a night's sleep.

We phoned the house and said that we were coming back. We would catch the train from Dorking to Redhill and then change and get the train to Merstham on Saturday morning and would that be all right and could we be accommodated, which of course it was. We duly turned up on Rockshaw Road before lunch where I was promptly collared by my father. "Good, I'm glad you've arrived because I'm a man short on the cricket team for the game this afternoon and you will do very nicely as a fill in." Forever after, Gig maintained that I had arranged that with my father before we left on the honeymoon and she would never believe me when I claimed it was purely fortuitous. I didn't even know that there was a cricket match that afternoon. But she would never believe me! So I played and she came down with Mother and Sonia and the other spectators and enjoyed an afternoon of village cricket, which she hadn't really seen before.

Once the game was over, the teams and the spectators were walking across the fields to get back to the road and my father was walking with one of the good ladies of the village

My brother Norman, me, Gig and my sister Sonia.

called Rosie Nicholson. He explained that Gig, who was a little bit in front of them, was Derrick's new wife to which Rosie replied, "Well, I haven't yet met her, but looking from here, I can certainly certify that she has a pair of very pretty ankles," and since my father was a connoisseur of ankles, he was greatly pleased.

    The seven days' leave came to an end and on the Tuesday morning I departed by train from Merstham for London and on to the little town of Fakenham in Norfolk, at which point I hoped I would be collected by one of the battery trucks to be taken back to the gun position and our encampment. This all happened as planned and I found that nothing very much had changed since I left a week before. We were now entering that period of the year from the first of September until winter when it was considered the most likely time for the Germans to invade if that was what they had in mind. Consequently, everything was at a state of maximum readiness for the anticipated onslaught. Maximum readiness was a pretty pathetic proposition in itself, considering that we only had those old six-inch naval guns, which had to cover a sector of the coast. This was fine in the middle and outwards for a bit left and right, but we couldn't reach the extreme ends of our sector. We didn't have the range in the guns. Ordnance maps are an essential part of artillery control and firing and the only one we had was the little domestic one produced by the ordnance survey parties but only at the scale of one mile to the inch. What we really needed was 10 miles to the inch. Consequently, my daily occupation for some period in September was using the small-scale map to produce by hand, the bigger version so that we might have a better chance of putting a shell where we wanted it.

Eventually the asthma with which I had been plagued since childhood caused my downfall. After I had paid a couple of visits to what was known as an MDS, a Main Dressing Station, with quite acute attacks, the army decided that they required my services no longer, and I was sent on leave pending discharge at the end of October 1940. So we were all at the Georgian House until my discharge came through, which was not until the early part of 1941. There was a further delay while we had to find passage for the two of us on a westbound boat, passengers being a not very important part of what the boats carried. By Christmas 1940, the threat of invasion had become somewhat remote and service leave was more easily obtained; my brother, who celebrated his 21st birthday on the 20th of December, managed to get a period of leave for that time and we duly celebrated with a good party and a dance at the house.

Finally, Gig and I left for Newfoundland in February 1941 on the steamship Bayano, which had been built as a banana carrier to bring bananas to the U.K. from the West Indies. She was fairly fast for the day but she was built to sail in tropical waters, which was not ideal for passage across the North Atlantic in winter. She carried us safely across to Halifax in spite of a couple of nights when the convoy was attacked by U-boats and several ships were sunk. After the third night of attack by U-boats, the Commodore, who was on board the

Gig and me at the Georgian House, waiting for my discharge to come through, 1940.

Bayano, decided that because we were far enough west and the position of the convoy was known to the submarines anyway, that it would be the right time to disperse the convoy and let each ship make its own way as best it could to wherever it was heading in North America. The chief engineer of the Bayano, who was the same size, shape and character as an actor called Will Fife, promptly announced to any passenger who was willing to listen that the Bayano engines were going to go flat out and that the engines would probably arrive in Halifax before the rest of the boat. Anyway, both boat and engines and everybody arrived safely at that destination. In Halifax we passed through Customs, collected all our baggage and arranged our passage by train to North Sydney to connect with the ferry to Port aux Basques. We left the luggage in charge of a redcap at Halifax station who was to put it on the train for Sydney. Unfortunately he put it on the train for Montreal and when we later appeared in the evening to catch the Sydney train we found no luggage of any kind whatever. We set off for Sydney and managed to get across on the ferry, onto the train and finally wound up in St. John's having only what we had on our backs. After some fuss and a delay of some days, the luggage finally appeared. We stayed first at 24 Monkstown Rd., Gig's mother's house, and after we had organized some furniture for ourselves, we moved into 78 Cochrane St. This was a house that also belonged to Gig's mother, which she usually leased out but the lease was about to end and we could move in.

While I had been away, my Uncle Eric had been appointed as the representative of the Minister of War Transport in the United Kingdom and he had departed from Bowring Brothers' office to the top floor of the Newfoundland Hotel, where he set up shop and was established next door to the Royal Canadian Navy Headquarters, with whom he had to work in close association. He had also taken with him his secretary, one of Bowring Brothers' accountants and the chief engineer of the Imogene (the ship had been lost) to act as a surveyor for him in relation to ship repairs, which were a common occurrence. The shops were running themselves with Walter Wills still in charge and the main business of the day was the ships' agency work under Geoffrey Milling, a director who had joined the company when Edgar Bowring, Jr. returned to England in 1936. Geoff was heavily involved with looking after the requirements of the end-

The Imogene sinking after she hit Canso Rock and a rope tangled in her propeller, 1940.

less merchantmen who were in and out of the harbour with damage caused either by the enemy or by heavy weather, for they were at sea for long periods. I was attached to him to assist in that sort of work. The shops really did not need much attention since there were shortages of everything and whatever merchandise one could obtain from suppliers pretty well sold itself. There was no seal fishery; the Imogene and Beothic had been lost at sea in 1940. Fish prices were high and, as usually happened in wartime, employment in Newfoundland was as high as it had ever been especially when American bases were being built on land that had been leased to the U.S.A. in St. John's, Stephenville and Argentia. St. John's itself was a naval base for the Atlantic escort ships and the place was alive with Royal Navy and Royal Canadian Navy ships and crews. There were many facilities to entertain and bring some degree of comfort to their crews and Gig was very busy at this work, as were many other members of the St. John's community.

The harbour of St. John's during the war was a most remarkable sight. The Navy had taken over the full length of the Southside wharves with the single exception of our Mudge's premises at the far west end, which was on property actually owned by the Admiralty, but which they could not use since the water depth at that end was too shallow for any naval vessels and was being used by schooners and other smaller ships. The Southside wharves over the course of time were rebuilt in a truly magnificent way and were eventually connected to the road system, which had not been the case before. Bowring's machine shop and forge were taken over by the navy and operated in the usual way but this time by naval shipwrights and machinists. The naval escorts docked at the Southside wharf and, towards the end of the war, there were additional finger piers constructed in the northwest corner for the newer naval vessels that had then become available and which made up the fast, well-armed, larger destroyers and frigates. These were not used as escorts but were support squadrons that could launch attacks on submarines that were harassing convoys. They only appeared in the final year or so of the war. They were built in the vicinity of Hickman's and Steer's wharves and the area is now covered by Harbour Drive. The Furness Withy and Harvey's piers were permanently occupied by merchant vessels of one sort or another, some of them actually discharging or loading cargo, but in many cases they were simply vessels that were in for repairs because of enemy action or the stress of weather. The remaining northside wharves were not much use in the war as they were small, short finger piers used normally for Labrador schooners and coastal vessels. They continued in this role for most of the time.

The water of the harbour was where the merchant vessels were anchored and usually the whole water area was covered with such boats. It was difficult to have them placed where they could avoid swinging into one another should there be a change in the wind and eventually a series of mooring buoys were placed down the centre line of the harbour from east to west; in between them, vessels could moor fore and aft abreast of each other, three or four between any given pair of buoys, which improved the arrangement considerably. The dry dock always had one or two vessels under repair. Some of the smaller vessels could be taken at the same time, one sitting on the chocks astern of the other. During the course of the war, a further emergency haul-out was established at Bay Bulls to take care of vessels that were not too great in size. Many of the merchant ships in the harbour had belonged to what at first were neutral nations, but during the course of the war they found that the Germans had overrun their countries and they were, therefore, vessels without a homport and were swallowed up into the Allied convoys and the general war effort. Some of these supposedly neutral countries became distinctly belligerent. Others just let everything pass over their heads without much comment. There were quite a few Greek ships that were a rather distressing lot for the vessels had usually not been maintained in very good order and required a good deal of repair and care. Others, like the Norwegians, were thoroughly fit for sea and their crews were more willing to sail them in order to help the Allied effort. There was the odd French vessel as well as some that were still strictly neutral, for example, Swedish vessels, but they found that they were better off sailing in Allied convoys than struggling around on their own, for the submarines mainly were concerned with sinking everything they could find, regardless of flag.

There were one or two amusing incidents connected with these foreign vessels. On one occasion, the dockyard held a small French vessel and astern of her there was a Greek ship. One evening, both crews were leaving their ships by the gangway to go ashore for an evening's entertainment. It resulted in a brawl of some magnitude with knives being brandished and a lot of fisticuffs and shouting. Neither one of the crews could understand the language of the other. The police had to be called and most of the two crews wound up in the local lockup. It just happened that Bowring's were agents for both of these ships and,

St. John's Harbour, c. 1941.

on the following morning, Geoffrey Milling had both captains in his office to find out what it was all about and what had to be done to bail the crews out of the clink. He asked one of the captains, "Well, how did the fight start?" and the version he received was that when one of the crews, I think the Greek one, came ashore and the sailors were walking along the dockside towards the road, they passed the French ship, which had its national flag flying on the stern flagpole; there was some chatter and apparently somebody heard the phrase "Fuck-a-da-flag" and that's when the fight started.

Vessels that had been repaired and were ready for sea were also in the harbour awaiting their call to join the next available convoy to take them either east or west. The normal arrangement was for an eastbound convoy to collect all the ships plus its escort in Halifax Harbour and Bedford Basin. The convoy then set sail eastward accompanied by the escort from Halifax to a point off Cape Race where ships from St. John's could join the group, and where the Atlantic escort, coming from St. John's harbour, would take over the escort duties and the Halifax escort would take a westbound convoy going back to Halifax or further west. Ships that were ready to leave St. John's usually heard about their departure time the day before they were to sail, which meant they had one more night in port and with certain neutrals, it was considered advisable to put a naval armed guard on board to make sure that the crew did not allow their windlass, which they would need to raise their anchor, to freeze. If the windlass froze, the crew would be unable to raise the anchor and thus would miss the convoy and could wait for another week or two or more safely anchored in St. John's harbour. It did not apply to all vessels but there were always one or two and the navy seemed to know who was going to be troublesome.

Another interesting point arose during the latter part of the war when the manager of the dockyard came to my Uncle Eric, who had to authorize most of the work that the dockyard did, and suggested to him that he could do some jobs more quickly if the harbour was equipped with a floating crane of some size. This meant that he would be able to do some repairs to any given vessel and thus save the problem of getting it on dry dock, which was where the main delay occurred. Vessels simply sat waiting for their turn on the dry dock, which was not very large. The dockyard manager said that he knew of an available crane but did not have the money to buy it; he thought that perhaps my uncle, representing the Ministry of War Transport, could persuade the Commissioner of the Commission of Government that the Newfoundland Government should buy the crane and make it available to the dry dock. My uncle agreed with this proposal and went to have a word with Sir Wilfrid Woods, who was the Commissioner of Public Utilities and who was in charge of the Newfoundland Dockyard. This was part of the Newfoundland Railway system, which he also ran. Sir Wilfrid inquired how much the crane would cost. My uncle replied that it would cost $375,000.

"Oh my Lord," said Sir Wilfrid, "I couldn't find that kind of money and it would take months to get permission from the Dominions Office to authorize that sort of payment above and beyond our present budget."

"Oh, well that's all right," said my uncle, "I'll buy it, on behalf of the Ministry of War Transport."

"You mean to say," said Sir Wilfrid, "that you can do that without further reference to anybody?"

"Certainly," replied Uncle Eric, "That's exactly why they have me here, to authorize things quickly and get them done, to get ships repaired and get on with the war effort, so don't you worry about it, I'll get the crane." And he did.

I think this incident illustrates more clearly than anything else that I know of, the problems that the Commission of Government had in doing a successful job in administering and improving Newfoundland's economic prospects. They brought honesty and generally good administration to the country but they were permanently short of funds and found it very difficult to wheedle any more out of the United Kingdom even for obviously good causes.

Our Mudge's premises were of no value to the navy so we used them for a thriving little shipbuilding industry making lifeboats to replace those of merchant vessels that had been damaged or lost at sea. Local shipwrights built many of these lifeboats and I found myself as the sort of general overseer of the operation. Not that I knew anything about building clinker built lifeboats but I made some useful efforts to keep the yard supplied with the necessary timber, metalwork and so forth. A lovely old Newfoundland seafarer known to all and sundry as Uncle Tom Hodder was in charge of the actual construction and ensured that the lifeboats were very well and soundly made. He had been a seaman all his life and still, with all the skills he had, he could not read or write. It was only during the term of the Commission of Government that education became compulsory in Newfoundland and then the schools were run on the denominational system, which was hardly helpful to the overall cause. The situation had arisen from the fact that, for many years, government, such as it was, did not provide for education and the churches found themselves called upon to establish their own schools where the population was sufficiently large enough. One has to credit the churches with showing a considerable degree of responsibility.

Reverting to the lifeboats, I remember a bit of an argument with my uncle as to whether Bowring Brothers was entitled to make a modest profit on the lifeboats or whether they were to be handed over at cost as being our contribution to the war effort. I believe I lost that argument and patriotism won.

And so time passed until May 25th, 1942, when our firstborn son arrived in the middle of the night. The 24th of May had been the expected day and, therefore, I had to remain at home instead of going on the usual 24th of May trouting expedition with two or three friends. Not only did I miss this enjoyable occasion, but the temperature on the 24th was in the 80-85 degree Fahrenheit range, which for this province was virtually unheard of. However, I took Gig up to the Grace Hospital as requested on the evening of the 24th and then returned to 78 Cochrane S. The Grace had no need to have me hanging around and I had no intention of doing so. Later that night I had a call from the hospital to say that himself had arrived and he was all complete and looked like a nice little boy, weighing somewhere between seven and eight pounds. I cabled my parents in England to say their first grandchild had arrived. The only consolation for missing the fishing trip was to find out that my colleagues, who had naturally gone off without me, had arrived on the river or pond only to discover when they unpacked the car that they had left their rods behind and thus they had no fishing either. One of their rods, which had been left propped up on the fence outside the owner's house, had, in the interval, been stolen. The other fishermen were my brother-in-law, Harvey Cole, and two good friends, Bill Knowling and Lewis Ayre.

Hand-tinted photo of R.C.A.F. Flight Observer David Baird, c. 1941. He had been holding a cigarette in his right hand but Em Baird didn't like it and had the photographer remove it during the touch-up and tinting.

On May 30th, while Gig was still in the hospital, that unwanted telegram was delivered to her mother saying that Mun Baird was missing as a result of air operations and that further information would come when they knew more about it. The telegram came from Canadian defence headquarters since Mun was in the RCAF, and I therefore cabled my father in England to see if it was possible for him to glean further information. His reply, after a day or so, said that Mun had been on the first 1,000-bomber raid over Cologne and that the plane had been damaged to such an extent that, as they were flying over the North Sea on the way back, the pilot, thinking he was bound to crash, ordered the crew to leave by parachute and give themselves a chance of being saved while he kept the plane in the air for as long as he could. Mun, being the observer or navigator, was one of those who jumped out. The plane managed to crash land on an English beach. The pilot was saved from the wreckage as well as the tail gunner, who had been unable to escape from his jammed turret. The rest of the crew were never heard from again. As a result, Mun's name is now engraved on a panel of the Air Force Memorial at Runnymede on the Thames; years later, his mother and Gig attended the opening ceremonies over which the Queen presided. There are over 50,000 names on this Memorial, which is dedicated to those who have no known grave. Our new and still unnamed infant, therefore, became David Monroe Bowring.

During the war we encountered many officers and men and it turned out that, in quite a number of cases, we had some connection with them even though we were not aware of it at the time when we first met. I remember having a visit in the office from a Lt. Hal Rack whose father had quite a connection with C.T. Bowring and Company in the oil business and when he saw the Bowring name, he thought he would make contact and see if we could help him in any way. One of the things he was after, since he was a keen dinghy sailor, was to know whether there might be something available that he could sail on the harbour while he was in port for a few days. It just happened that I had a 14-foot dinghy that Uncle Eric had given me for my 21st birthday and it was in storage up at the Mudge's premises. I made it available to him and he enjoyed it on the harbour on the different occasions when his corvette reappeared in St. John's. Later on when his vessel was moved to some other naval duty and he no longer came into St. John's, he was replaced by another naval lieutenant who had met Hal Rack and was told, "If you're going to St. John's, look up Derrick Bowring and Gig and they will look after you in whatever way you require." This was Peter Frith, who was stationed in St. John's as he was an electronics specialist and was in charge of the maintenance and repair of the Asdic submarine detection equipment on all the vessels in Newfoundland. He later became the man in charge of doing the same thing for the early models of radar. We came to know him well and when he was turfed out of some naval billet, which he didn't like, he came to board with us for a period of months so we knew him extremely well. In fact, he was staying with us in the early days of our son David being there. David was a notoriously poor sleeper and there were certainly one or two occasions when Gig and I were fast asleep while David was howling in the next room and keeping Frithy awake. So he would get up and walk him back and forth in the room, rock him to sleep, put him back to bed, and peace and quiet reigned once again. Next morning we heard several remarks about, "The things I do for England!"

Another visitor was David Fletcher, a young lieutenant on a corvette called HMS Primrose who called on me because he was an Old Salopian, an alumni of Shrewsbury School. He was one year junior to me but in the same House. He was in and out of St. John's for at least a year, possibly more, and on arrival would turn up at the house for a wash and brush-up and a little bit of non-naval food and we enjoyed his company very much. Unfortunately, I was never able to find what happened to him and the Old Salopian Club doesn't seem to have any record of what he did or didn't do after leaving the school. He wasn't lost at sea for HMS Primrose survived the war.

Another later visitor was Dacre Powell who came because, prior to the war, he had worked for about a year or so in the shipping department of C.T. Bowring and Company in London and it was obvious why he would make contact. He was a member of the crew of one of the American four-stackers, the old destroyers that the Americans had mothballed in the U.S. and traded to the United Kingdom in exchange for various bases in the West Indies, but not their bases in Newfoundland. For some reason they were allowed to use these as a free gift but I never knew why.

In the spring of 1943, St. John's had a visit from HMS Sandwich as part of the convoy escort; this was the same ship that had rescued Gig and the crew of the Geraldine Mary in 1940. Many of the crew were the same, including the captain, and on May 24th, I was able to take him and one other with a couple of friends of mine on the May 24th trouting expedition. The weather lived up to its usual Newfoundland reputation for that date and as we fished for trout we also enjoyed a snowstorm, which rather astonished the captain and put him off his fishing. I don't think we caught very many fish for it was not only snowing, it was cold and windy. However, on the way back to HMS Sandwich, we repaid some of the debt owing for rescuing my wife.

I think it was some time in 1943 that, at the urging of Geoffrey Milling, we began to talk about acquiring a machine for bookkeeping. This led to quite an entertaining debate because Walter Wills was dead set against it. He couldn't see any machine taking the place of men equipped with pens and writing in ledgers and keeping track of the business in all aspects where one could see it written down on a piece of paper. Walter was ultimately responsible for granting credit, not only to individuals in St. John's and area, but for wholesale credit to dealers all around the island and, in his mind, no machine was capable of keeping up with that. Because of the war, bookkeeping machines, at least new ones, were hard to acquire but eventually we did find a rebuilt model, a Burroughs machine that came from Butler Brothers who were the Burroughs agents in St. John's.

This activity was followed by the arrival of Jim Cantley, a man whom Geoff had known when he was with the Hudson's Bay Company. Jim had been with The Bay and was a qualified fur trader and colour expert, adept at determining the price of a fur based on its colour. Before the war, he had left The Bay and had been in touch with Geoff Milling. C.T. Bowring and Co. were interested in the fur trade because of our activities in sealing and the resulting seals that had to be marketed, and this interest culminated in C.T. Bowring and Company forming a subsidiary called the Baffin Trading Company Ltd., with Jim Cantley as its managing director. The company established one or more fur trading outlets in northern Labrador and northern Quebec. These ceased operations with the coming of the war and that put poor old Cantley out of business.

He understood the workings of bookkeeping and bookkeeping machines so he was brought down to set up the system for Bowring Brothers. Since my uncle had disappeared into the Newfoundland Hotel with his Ministry of War Transport, his office at Water Street was empty and Jim Cantley was established there to draw up the necessary directions and produce the paperwork and the forms needed for this new machine bookkeeping venture. The poor man was looked upon with a good deal of hostility from all the bookkeepers and certainly from Walter Wills, who had no use for him whatsoever, and I assume that the chief accountant, Bertie Shears, was not overly enamoured.

While Walter Wills remained working and with the company, we virtually had two systems of bookkeeping, one on the machine and the old one that he refused to abandon as far as the accounts receivable were concerned. This went on until Walter retired in the spring of 1944 and I landed up with the shops. His final comment to me was, "You will feel very small the day after I leave," so I didn't doubt that I would.

Well, the next day came and I didn't feel particularly small but I wondered what I was going to do with four department managers who were so old – 72, 75, 76 and 79 – and I was 28 and there was no pension plan for anyone! The problem arose because Walter Wills had been a department manager himself and he realized that no department manager wanted any director interfering in his departmental affairs. Walter himself, when he became a director, took care not to disturb the peace and quiet of any of the departments or to ruffle the manager, provided things were going along in a satisfactory way and provided he, as the responsible director, could maintain control over the granting of credit. So the war continued and conditions were what they were. There was really nothing much I could do but let things run the same way. Walter had been my mentor and I understood his philosophy, but at the same time, the war was bringing a sea change in management and human resource structures and I was determined that somehow, at some time, pensions would exist.

Credit during the war was not a real problem. There was nothing adrift because there was very high employment in Newfoundland; people were prosperous and bad debts were not a matter for grave concern. Therefore, I just let the stores run on their usual basis and everything seemed to run smoothly with whatever merchandise we were able to obtain and sell to the public. I occupied some of my time in brawling with the minions of the Commission of Government who were planning and then setting about installing price controls, which caused a certain amount of commotion amongst the wholesale and retail trade. The Commission of Government members, and even the civil servants in the Finance Department, didn't really understand very much about wholesale markup, retail markup or the problem of mark-downs. That occupied my time in a moderately useful way while I let things idle along on their own.

Meanwhile, in the shipping world, the Ranger had been lost. At this point I can't remember how, but I think it was a question of heavy seas and she was abandoned; I know the crew was rescued. The Terra Nova had been chartered to some of the U.S. base contractors who were building what ultimately turned out to be the airbase in Thule in Greenland. The Terra Nova carried cargoes of equipment and building materials for the base and, of course, being strengthened for ice, she could do it at any time of year that it was possible to get there. Unfortunately, on her way from Thule, she was caught and ultimately crushed by the ice but all her crew were rescued by the U.S. Coast Guard.

SS Eagle in St. John's Harbour, c. 1939.

We now had only the SS Eagle left and, believe it or not, she was chartered to make a voyage to the Antarctic to carry down the equipment and supplies for a weather station at some remote spot. All this in the cause of the Allied needs in wartime, and so she set off south with a Captain Sheppard in command and her redoubtable old bosun, Tom Carroll, who must have been in his very late 80s. The Eagle carried out the job successfully and reappeared in St. John's. The Eagle and the Terra Nova were the only ships of ours that penetrated that far south, the Terra Nova having done it on the Scott Expedition in 1912.

Early in December 1943, a cable from my parents told me that my brother Norman was missing on air operations over Germany, and shortly after that came another cable saying that he had been killed. This was a double blow as he and I had corresponded about the possibility of him joining me in Newfoundland after the war, and once more we would be back to Bowring Brothers, the original formation of the company. Equally, it was a blow in that I had lost a much loved brother, the companion of my youth with whom I had enjoyed a number of escapades, games of golf and other things one enjoys when young. Norman was an athlete to his fingertips and any game that involved a ball was grist to his mill, whether it was football, cricket, golf, squash, fives or tennis; if a ball was involved, that was his meat and he excelled at virtually all of them.

My father, like my brother, was a great wielder of bat and ball and sport of all kinds appealed to him strongly. He was a very good cricketer and he and Norman, between them, established a record that I do not think has yet been broken at Shrewsbury School. In 1936 and 1937, Norman played cricket for the School First Eleven and my father was on the Old Salopian team that played against the school. I think in the 1937 game, my father, who was fielding in the slips, made what he described as the best catch of his life only to discover that he had dismissed his son. He said, "I could easily have dropped it and it would not have looked deliberate." In 1938, after Norman had left school, they played together on the same team as Old Salopians against whatever First Eleven the school had that year. It hadn't been done before and I don't think it's been achieved since.

Norman and Cyril Bowring after a cricket match, c. 1937.

It was only at golf that I could keep pace with Norman and that was partly because he was rather more erratic. I recall that in our teens we used to practise our seven- and eight-iron shots by one of us standing on the tennis court behind the house and the other across the road in a farmer's field. We would then loft the ball from one to the other, clearing the roof of the house as we did so. The house, incidentally, was three storeys and one really had to lift the ball to a considerable height. We did this for ages to our great enjoyment and we never broke a window, though we did smash a few roof tiles.

The other incident I particularly recall involving Norman had to do with a small pigeon loft that existed at the bottom of our garden where some homing pigeons lived. It was a small sort of aviary type structure standing on a concrete floor with roosts for the birds at the back of it and an open area with wire around it in which they could fly around during the daytime. Most of the time they could enter and leave as they wished, but if you wanted to catch a particular pigeon for a pigeon race, which were held locally quite frequently, then you could shut the trapdoor and keep the pigeon in until you could catch him. He would then be carted off to France where he would fly back to you and could enter the house once more.

We were looking at it one day and decided, from various signs such as holes in the ground that seemed to lead up underneath the concrete, that there were rats living under it and that we ought to eliminate them. First of all we tried with our dog who was an expert rat catcher, but when he didn't make any progress digging, we decided that perhaps a few buckets of water poured down the holes might flush the rats out. Again, failure, and nothing happened.

So we then had a really bright idea and returned to the house to get a package of what was called carbide, which was something that you used in those days to give you a light on your bicycle if you were riding in the dark. You would put the carbide, a sort of gritty stuff, in the base of the lamp and then add water to produce a gas that would burn and give you a faint religious light – not much use for you to see by but it at least let other traffic realize that something was there on the road. We brought the carbide and stuffed it down a hole. We thought that the gas would be enough to deal with the rats. We could see the sort of white plumes of gas floating around down there but unfortunately that didn't produce any rats either. However, we realized that the gas was used with a match and would light, so perhaps a flame would stir things up. As a result of this brilliant thought, we lit a match and threw it down one of the rat holes. Instantly the whole contraption, birds and all, rose about six inches in the air, including the concrete floor, with a resounding bang. The only visible damage was that we had cracked the concrete floor but miraculously everything came back almost in its original position, and when the dust settled, it looked just as it had when we started. We decided that silence was the best policy and apart from jokingly telling it to my children, this is the first official recording of this momentous event in our joint youth.

Norman had started the war in the Territorial Army, in the Queen's Own Royal West Surrey Regiment, but his battalion had not been sent to France and so he was not involved in any Dunkirk heroics and he had really become exceedingly bored with hanging around England supposedly guarding a bridge for no apparent reason. Presumably he was protecting it against parachutists being dropped in the area, which of course, never happened, and eventually he discovered that he could transfer to the Royal Air Force and train to be an airman. He wound up as a flying officer in Bomber Command and eventually he was the pilot and skipper of a Lancaster bomber and a member of 405 Squadron, which was a Pathfinder squadron, one of the more dangerous activities in Bomber Command.

Number 405 Squadron, which still exists based in Greenwood, Nova Scotia, was a Royal Canadian Air Force squadron and in those days squadrons could be made up of Canadians,

British, New Zealanders, Australians. They were all mixed in together. Norman had several Englishmen in his crew and one Canadian. They seemed to be a happy bunch, but if you were a Pathfinder you were over the target area for much longer than anybody else and you were, so to speak, looking for trouble. Sadly, they found it. His grave is in the Commonwealth War Graves cemetery in the middle of Berlin on what was, and still is, called the Preussenallee.

My sister and I, each with our eldest child, visited his grave on the 50th anniversary of his death and attended the Remembrance Day service in the cemetery and later in the English church in that area, which used to be the church of the British Embassy in Berlin. It was an interesting occasion to be there, in the capital of Germany, on one of the main streets in Berlin surrounded by the British Army, the army of Occupation after the war. I hoped Hitler was looking down on it.

R.A.F. Flying Officer Norman Bowring (back row, second from left) with his 405 Squadron crew, c. 1942.

CHAPTER FIVE
THE MODERN AGE OF RETAIL

By the end of 1944, with the war obviously drawing to an end, with Walter Wills retired, and with my uncle coming back from his work as the representative of the Ministry of War Transport, I decided that I would like to find somebody to join me in the operation of the shops; someone who would, in time, be qualified to be on the board and would, to some extent, even up the unequal distribution of responsibilities among the directors.

I don't remember when I was actually elected to the Board of Directors because I had been attending board meetings, which were pretty infrequent, in the capacity of company secretary for a considerable amount of time. The job had previously been held by Walter Wills, who was only too pleased to relinquish it. It was Walter's brilliant idea that I could be made company secretary, allowing him to escape from it, and it would be a good excuse to pay me for doing that extra work since Laurence Stoddart had done me out of money that I had been told I would receive before I left England. At some point during that period, I was elected to the board.

Armed with the board's approval, I set about compiling a short list of possible candidates in order to submit one name to the board. In my own mind, I knew that I wanted a Newfoundlander, someone roughly my own age but also someone who had had experience and some time spent out of Newfoundland in other parts of the world. Finally I arrived at two preferred names and referred them to my chief personnel consultant, to wit, my wife! I always found that she could take an objective view to this sort of question and after careful thought, would give me not only her decision, but the reasons for it and why in her opinion so-and-so would be the best man or woman. She never failed me in the answer of any such question that I might ask, particularly when it had to do with people. Our selection was Fred Ayre, whom I have mentioned previously as having been at Shrewsbury with me in the early '30s. He had been in another House and was about a year older than me, but during our careers at the school we had encountered one another in the same form occasionally. Although I couldn't say that I knew him well, I certainly knew him well enough to appreciate that he was both highly intelligent and industrious. I knew he wanted to get back to Newfoundland and had built up experience that we needed. After going to Cambridge from Shrewsbury, he had worked for one of the Coca-Cola branches in England and had experience of commercial activity prior to the war. He served for the entire duration of the war – the full five years plus. I believe he was the longest serving Canadian during the war who wasn't in the regular army. I wrote to him and I think addressed it to an army post office in

Greece, for that is where he still was in the last days of the war and, after a certain amount of delay, I received a reply saying that he would very much like to accept the offer and would join us as soon as he could achieve his demobilization.

The situation then was that I was nominally in charge of a small family department store exactly the same as family department stores found in endless country towns in England and in small towns across Canada. The only difference being that Bowring Brothers sold not only at the retail level, but had an extensive business at the wholesale level supplying dealers around the island, on the coasts and in the interior, which all led to very extensive credit having to be granted for very lengthy periods. This was an evil that normal small family department stores avoided, but in Newfoundland it was impossible to evade. Business was also complicated by the fact that the company was quite heavily involved in the handling of fish for export; cod oil for tanking, repacking and exporting; the provision of salt in bulk to fishermen for drying codfish; the seal fishery, which was a major enterprise for the company; and for various other dealings in whatever produce was available on the island for export. The whole thing was a more complicated affair than purely department store operating, even if small. In addition, the company acted as agents for the Liverpool, London and Globe Insurance Company who could write policies for fire and accidents and so forth, and the company was rather proud of being the Newfoundland agents for Lloyd's of London, the underwriting organization that was so well known throughout the world.

Yours truly with Fred Ayre, 1952.

The board had approved the invitation to Fred Ayre and my uncle was really particularly keen on it because he thought well of him and knew he was intelligent. It gave him additional pleasure because he was the great-grandson of Robert Ayre, who originally came to Newfoundland as the first apprentice that Benjamin Bowring employed, and the Ayre family had gone on to greater things after Robert had learned his trade from Benjamin B. They were in the retail business on a rather bigger scale than Bowring Brothers but they kept themselves strictly away from fish, cod oil, seals or anything else. It seemed appropriate that a descendant of Robert Ayre's should return to the fold and do a bit of good for Bowring Brothers and as the years unfolded, he most certainly did. He wound up as chairman, succeeding me, and made a very substantial contribution to the welfare of the company in the years to come.

Twenty Castle Street, Liverpool, had always been the head office of C.T. Bowring and Company Limited and it was the office to which Bowring Brothers reported over the years. However, in the early 1930s Sir Frederick Bowring, who was the chairman, died and was succeeded by his brother Sir Edgar R. Bowring. He lived in London and so London became the head office and remained that way to the end. Bowring Brothers continued for some years to report to Liverpool. I had in my own mind decided that I must find some way of bringing our department store activities and the way the store functioned up to date. I felt sure that the way in which we operated, where everything depended on the department manager attending to every little thing from buying the stock, to hiring the staff, to marking up what he sold, maintaining the gross profit and producing a net profit, was not the way a modern store should operate. A possible exception was the dry goods department, which did have an experienced assistant manager who was quite capable of doing the same work, and did so insofar as the actual manager trusted him. I had no idea and needed help in finding out how to achieve this desirable objective. Consequently, I wrote to Edgar R. Bowring, Jr., who had, until 1936, worked in St. John's and in that year had moved back to Liverpool. He was now the senior man there and since that was the office to which Bowring Brothers reported I would ask him for help. As is quite common in cities with large commercial interests and activities, a great many of their directors and senior management would be members of clubs to which they would adjourn each day for a bit of gossip and their lunch. Edgar belonged to such a club and there he met, as a fellow member, one Duncan Norman, incidentally an Old Salopian but an Old Salopian of enormous importance to Bowring Brothers.

Duncan Norman was the chairman and managing director of a company called Owen Owen Limited, which operated a chain of department stores, two of which were in Liverpool, and others in nearby northern towns. The fact that he was approached by an Old Salopian made quite a difference to him and the knowledge that the Bowring stores in St. John's, Newfoundland, were in need of help and advice appealed to him in particular, because in his own activities he had been eyeing Canada as a place in which he would like to expand his business. At the same time that these discussions were going on in Liverpool, I managed to find a way of reaching England. This was by way of one of Bowater's paper carriers, since after the war there was no shipping that offered passenger service and flying was difficult and required priority access. I duly arrived in Tilbury, on the Thames, aboard the SS Corner Brook, having been 10 days in crossing the ocean from Port aux Basques. During my stay in

England, I went up to Liverpool and met Duncan for lunch, with Edgar present, and later I visited him in his office and went into greater detail of the problems I was facing.

Miraculously, all my problems were answered by the generosity of Duncan Norman and his people at Owen Owen in Liverpool. They could not have done more for us, nor could they have given help in any greater way than what resulted from my visit and talk with him. After our initial discussions, it was agreed that I would send two men to Owen Owen who would be able to absorb whatever their personnel could teach. They would come back to St. John's and put into practice whatever was the right way to run the store and the methods of doing it. I obviously sent Fred Ayre as one of them, and another man. The second was a poor choice and he soon returned to St. John's. I had not realized at the time the level of education that was required for the man to fully comprehend this training. It was my fault and I regretted it, but still, Fred Ayre more than made up for us being short one man. Fred was over in England for probably a month or six weeks, took voluminous notes on how things were run in a department store, learned about the retail inventory methods of which we had never heard, and came back remarkably well equipped to instill the systems into Bowring Brothers.

After his time in Liverpool with Owen Owen Limited, his first problem was to introduce and explain to me how they operated the retail inventory system and how they were organized to carry out the various activities that were necessary in a department store. We didn't really have to debate whether or not we were going to use the system, it was more a question of how we were going to install it in the operation that already existed, how the various people that would be needed were going to be found, and how and when we would introduce it. It seemed obvious that since we would be taking a physical inventory anyway at the end of December 1946, it would be logical to start the new scheme on the first of January 1947. We would then have some months in which to make the planned changes in the organization and get ourselves geared up for what was going to be a major shake-up in the store. First of all, it was obvious that the two departments that would have to be part of the new organization were the dry goods and hardware departments. These covered everything from ladies' fashions and men's, women's and children's clothing to house furnishings, housewares and hardware. The retail grocery department and the retail store (the one department that only sold wholesale) were not involved, and we thankfully put them aside to carry on in their own inimitable way in the coming year. The old managers of the dry goods and hardware departments had recently retired and the two departments were being run temporarily by senior personnel already in the department. We therefore had a free hand at reorganizing the overall management and deciding how the whole store would be run and what the arrangements and breakdown of departments would be for the future. We discussed the overall organization of the Owen Owen stores and then had to decide how far we could fit that type of arrangement into our much smaller operation. It meant the creation of certain new positions and the elimination of others. The previously omnipotent department manager jobs would disappear and we would install a totally new slate of management. An overall store manager would be concerned with the daily running of the store and the organization and general supervision of its various functions. Then we needed a personnel manager to take care of employment, training and so forth. An equipment manager would look after all the physical equipment, from the buildings down to the delivery vans and the cash registers, stationery, etc. As for the sales departments themselves, we would divide the previous big departments into numerous smaller ones, and because of the variety of merchandise that we had to carry in our relatively small store, these departments would be further subdivided into what we called sections, thus giving us a department manager who would control several sections and each section, in turn, would have its section head. In many cases this was simply the senior salesperson, or even just the one person in that section.

On the all-important buying side, we had to find suitably qualified individuals with sufficient experience in the merchandise involved to become buyers for, in most cases, several departments. The organization provided for information to flow up and down from salesperson to section head, to department manager, to buyer and back to the salesperson. Another important appointment that hadn't existed before was that of receiving room manager – the receiving room being the place in which all the merchandise coming in from suppliers would be received, physically checked and clearly marked with the selling price, date of arrival, a supplier's number and whatever other useful information was needed based on the particular merchandise. On the whole, the overall organization picture and the people to man the senior positions were decided by Fred Ayre and me, but everything else was discussed on as wide a scale as possible, particularly the breakdown into sections and departments, bearing in mind the individual salespeople who were available to become section heads and department managers. This took a great deal of thought and, in some cases, a bit of manoeuvring to keep everybody satisfied. After we had decided these major organizational matters, my part was to talk to the senior people who were to fill the new positions and explain to them what their responsibilities would be. Fred Ayre undertook the onerous task of writing out the job descriptions for each person, the overall organizational structure and how it was to be achieved. So, as far as we could arrange it, everybody in the store was made aware of what we were planning to do, how it was to happen and when it was going to happen. We also wanted to generally bring them up to a state of enthusiasm to get the job done efficiently and on time at the end of the old year and the beginning of the new. The store was still open for business on a daily basis and everything to the outside eye looked as though it was absolutely normal. Fred Ayre preferred to write all his job descriptions, work to be done and how it was to be carried out in longhand and then had them typed and revised before being issued to the people concerned. It was an enormous task and he settled down to do it in a most vigorous way – reams of paper appeared on my desk for comment and approval over the next few weeks.

At the same time, he took an interest directly in the activities of the store, especially in the direction of sales promotion, in which he was a complete expert and in which he probably had learned a good deal from his previous experience in England with the Coca-Cola company. At the same time, our old advertising manager had retired and Fred was able to take the assistant manager in hand and give him a lead as to what was going to happen in future. What happened woke Water Street up to the fact that something peculiar was going on down at Bowring's, which they hadn't fully realized before. The advertising took on a new look and was organized in a different way, not because the advertising manager told a department that he had booked so much space in *The Evening Telegram* and it was there to fill, but rather because the ads were based on the merchandise the departments wanted to advertise that also had good public appeal. Then advertisements that had never been seen over Bowring's name before suddenly appeared and attracted public attention. Our sales went up quite significantly.

With three elderly managers gone from the former dry goods, hardware and grocery departments, it became possible to take a more direct intervention in the running of the whole store. A few new applicants with a bit of ambition appeared and were employed as they realized that we were already shaking up the fairly lethargic routine of Water Street retailing and that they might have a more exciting future with us and possibly bigger earnings. On January 2nd, 1947, the new retail inventory system started under new management arrangements. More buyers, each with a small flock of departments and sections, new order forms in use, central receiving and marking, and prices established by buyers who had a target mark-up to be achieved. Fred Ayre was already showing an astonishing aptitude and understanding of the business of the shops and was a huge help to me in the sense that he was someone with whom I could discuss the future arrangements and expectations while fully grasping what I was talking about. Once we had agreed on a course of action, I had hardly any more to do before he had it all arranged and in operating condition. Life became much easier and, in addition, I had an ally who could explain to other directors exactly what we were up to and why, and how we hoped it would work. It is worth noting that we were the first people to install the retail inventory system in Newfoundland. Therefore, not a creature in the place knew anything about it, how it should function, or how it was operated. We were well ahead of our competitors. To aid Bowring's in installing the retail inventory system, Owen Owen sent out their chief statistician to guide us in producing the forms that would be needed and instructions as to how they were to be used, and I think that without that help, we would have had a much more difficult task than we had.

A full inventory was taken before we brought in the new system. Prior to taking the inventory, all stock that was considered to be held purely for wholesale purposes, had been transferred to a warehouse that we owned on Job Street and the wholesale establishment was set up under my old friend Heber Harnett, with whom I had made my original cross-country railway tour in 1936. At the same time, we had been making great efforts to modernize the sales floor by displaying more of the stock and making the merchandise readily available for customers to feel and examine, rather than having to wait for a salesman or saleswoman to bring it out and show it to a customer from behind a counter. One of the immediate things we were able to do was design a display fixture on which everything was completely open. It was made out of two sheets of 4 x 8 foot three-quarter inch plywood with a major display level at the lower part and a narrower one in the middle somewhat higher up. It worked extremely well and St. John's was surprised to find so much of our merchandise on display where they could feel things, hold them, try them, look at the price and then make up their mind as to whether it was suitable for them or not. It was a real revolution to Water Street shoppers. The fixture was inexpensive and simple to make and caused an interesting episode. A comparison shopper from Ayre and Sons came in armed with a tape measure to measure that particular fixture. Its fame seemed to have spread. To make it more entertaining, whoever was in charge of the sales floor at the time offered to hold one end of the tape for this individual, greatly to his embarrassment and our enjoyment.

At the time that all this was taking place on the sales floor, we were busily following a sizable rebuilding program. We were filling in empty space that existed within the whole block of our buildings. It didn't provide much extra space but it made communication within the building more simple, and it gave us some extra sales floor when every inch of such space was welcome. That search for space was to go on for some time as we endlessly sought more selling areas and, on one occasion, somewhat later than 1947, when we were doing some renovation work in one of the basement areas, we invited the architect we were using at the time to come down and let us know whether we could move a dividing wall. He took one look at it, ran for the stairs back up to ground level and told us not to touch that wall whatever we did. The building would collapse! We didn't touch it.

With all of these changes, we now had a personnel manager whose responsibility was to find suitable sales staff or utility staff for the different departments. In the past this had been done by the omnipotent department managers but we now had a personnel department that was responsible, not only for the hiring of suitable staff, but for their training as well. Up on the third floor were a series of small rooms that had years before been used by the Bowring family, Benjamin and his sons, where they lived and were raised as children. One of these smaller rooms was converted to a training room and was set up with counters, display fixtures, other fixtures against the wall and was generally made to look like a sales floor

> **BOWRING BROTHERS, Ltd**
>
> ST. JOHN'S, NEWFOUNDLAND
>
> — Established 1811 —
>
> GENERAL MERCHANTS and STEAMSHIP OWNERS
>
> Wholesale and Retail Dealers in
>
> Dry Goods, Hardware, Groceries and Ships' Stores
>
> Exporters of
>
> Codfish, Codoil, Cod Liver Oil, Seal Oil and Seal Skins.
>
> Agents for "Lloyd's" and Liverpool and London and Globe Insurance Company
>
> Iron or Wooden Sealing Ships suitable for Arctic or Antarctic exploration available for Charter
>
> Sportsmen who intend visiting Newfoundland will find no difficulty in selecting Guns, Ammunition, Fishing Tackle and Food Supplies from this firm.
>
> Address all Communications To **BOWRING BROTHERS, Ltd.,** St. John's, Newfoundland

Bowring's display ad, 1947.

in the main store. It was equipped with a certain amount of inventory on display and, under the guidance of the personnel manager, various skilful salespeople would demonstrate how to make a sale and how not to make a sale. I know the whole process created endless amounts of laughter. I attended one or two sessions and, really, you could understand why there was so much laughter because they had some of the staff acting the part of customers. Of course they knew how customers could act. Some were nice, some were not, some were helpful, some were difficult and they used to play the part of the different types of customer so that the new salespeople in training would know what to expect and how to deal with them. It was a good program and went on for quite a long period.

    The improved advertising, improved display arrangements, improved level of skill in the sales staff and the improved selection of merchandise available through our new methods it all contributed to a considerable increase in our sales and we indulged in different types of promotion. In past years we would never have thought of or even have considered that we were quite outside the normal run of advertising in St. John's. On one occasion when we had something particularly special to offer or a sale to announce, we had notices printed on small pieces of paper and, with several thousand of these "flyers" loaded into an old fashioned bi-plane that was stationed at the Torbay airport, we would have the pilot drop them over St. John's as rain from heaven. Fred Ayre, who was directly related to our next door competitors, Ayre and Sons, was heard to say, "That oughta give Uncle Jim another heart attack." That comment arose because his Uncle Jim was the senior director and chairman of Ayre and Sons and was inclined to feel that he needed a rest cure every now and then and would depart into a sick room in the Grace Hospital, upon which several of these pamphlets had fallen. There he would relax for a week or 10 days and, in the opinion of most people, pretend to be ill. I think it was more a pleasant relaxation in what Dr. Anderson, who used to be the chief medical officer of the Grace Hospital, once described as, "Oh the Grace Hospital, it's just like a first class outport boarding house."

Now that we had what you might call the show on the road, the next problem was how to control it and see if we could actually make some net profit. We expected to have a certain amount of trouble in keeping track of what, in the retail world, are known as reductions. If you carry your inventory at its selling price, every time you decide to reduce that selling price you have to record the value of the reduction in a separate reduction book. This then reduces the value of the inventory that you are carrying. It was only too easy to forget to do this when prices, in the excitement of a promotion, were altered downwards, and we knew trouble would be coming in that field and naturally it did.

Altogether, it was really great fun. We felt sure that we were now on the right track. We were steadily improving our methods and the whole system of management was progressing well. People who were newly appointed to their present jobs were beginning to find their feet more surely on the ground and were starting to seriously think about how they could improve one aspect or another of their field of responsibility. It was very encouraging to everybody and life at work became an enjoyable experience, rather than just a job. We were beginning to make considerably greater sales and these had to be coming to us at the expense of our competitors. From its normal reasonably soporific state, Water Street began to wake up and I can't say that they set about causing us any trouble; we really didn't notice any response to it. We did begin to be talked about amongst the buying public, however, and at some fairly early point, I think during 1947, we used the slogan, "Bowring's, Everybody's Store." People in the town when asked, "Where are you going?" responded, "Oh, I'm going to Everybody's." This became quite a familiar phrase in normal conversation and everybody knew that if you talked about Everybody's, it meant Bowring's and nothing else.

At the same time that this learning process was underway, three of the previously mentioned elderly department managers had retired under the scheme of pension that the company used at the time. This was to grant them as reasonable a pension as the company could afford. This was paid entirely out of Bowring Brothers' pocket as there was no pension scheme in existence to which the employees themselves had made any contribution. I had to use this method for quite a few more elderly members of the staff, who were either too old, or too stuck in their old-fashioned ways to cope with the new systems and the new methods that were soon going to descend upon them. This method of pensioning was a great burden on the company for many years to come because my uncle always contended that Bowring Brothers' pensioners lived forever.

So here we were in 1947, going through two enormous upheavals in the retail and wholesale part of the business. First was the converting of our retail business to the retail inventory method. In addition, during the same period we had to cope with the fact that Newfoundland was going to become a province of Canada, which would totally change the value of the stocks that we had in hand when Confederation actually occurred. Lurking in the background, as well, was my problem with our chief accountant and, by 1948, I simply had to sidetrack him by making him the company secretary and keeper of the seal and other historical activities, while we imported a new CA from England. I think the London office found him for us and that at least solved the problem of how the ledgers were going to cope with the retail inventory system.

Around the time of Walter Wills' retirement, I had realized that with all the elderly staff that we had in the shops, and no pension plan to take care of their retirement, it was essential that I seek some action that would correct the problem. It was about this time that life assurance companies were taking an interest in the pension business and they had early pension schemes available, however, on a very limited basis by modern standards. I was able after a certain amount of argument, to put a plan in place with one of the life assurance companies. It was with what was then called North American Life, which has since been swallowed up by bigger outfits. The plan could not take care of men who were older than 55 at the time the plan came into effect, which left us with quite a number of people who would have to be looked after out of the company's own pocket. For those under 55, a modest pension would be available for them at a retirement age of 65 and, in the case of women, a retirement age of 60. It is interesting and amusing, looking back on these early arrangements some years later. We ran into trouble with the law, which said that men and women had to be treated equally and have equal benefits. In our arrangement we had been trying to be kind to the ladies, but in the final event we found that the poor old girls had to do another five years' work to make them equal to the men's program. So much for chivalry!

This was a contributory plan with the employees contributing five per cent and the company putting in an equal amount, which, over the course of time, became considerably greater as we sought to bring pensions in line with inflation and the need to give a more reasonable percentage of final wages. One entertaining point was that my uncle thought it necessary that we defer our decision to start the plan to the parent company in London. The reply he received was approval of the plan with the one condition, that directors were not to be allowed into it! This was all very fine for the old boys who sat there in London, full of money and full of shares, who didn't need a pension under any circumstances. It was a different matter for the likes of us sitting in St. John's, who owned no shares, didn't have any money and in the course of time certainly needed an adequate pension, thank you very much.

It didn't take long to discover that the plan with a life assurance company couldn't really keep pace with the actual situation on the ground as people earned more money. Due to the fixed benefit arrangement, we finally sought actuarial advice and decided to operate our own plan with money put into our own fund and the investment undertaken by an investment manager. This was the ultimate and supremely more efficient system that we reached but it was still many years before we got to it. Every time we had the investment done, either by a trust company or by a life assurance company, they could not keep pace with the earnings that we required. It was in the early 1970s that I visited half a dozen potential investment managers in Toronto and finally made arrangements with one who understood exactly what our problem was. He would never run a pension plan for one company that was lumped into funds for other companies, on the basis that each pension plan required separate investment treatment, and that's what he and his partners would give it. When we made the change and paid the accumulated fund into our own operation, the monthly deductions for the plan were sent to the bank, the bank paid the broker the amount authorized by the investment manager and we never had any further trouble. In fact we accumulated surpluses from year to year, which enabled the pensions to be stepped up, even existing pensions, and satisfaction reigned all around. Plus Bowring Brothers' directors were included!

During most of 1947, I was struggling to build a house out on Portugal Cove Road, which would have been simple under normal circumstances, but the whole world was suffering from the aftereffects of the war and the materials needed for house building were either impossible to get, or you could only get part of what you needed. On one occasion, I had to go to an auction of some temporary army buildings that the Canadian Army had in Buckmaster's Field where I bid on two wooden buildings that Bowring's carpenters later demolished and the major planks were used for the rafters in the house. The radiators from these buildings were almost exactly what I needed to fit the various rooms in the house. Even the copper pipe and stuff that would normally be considered scrap was all pressed into service by carpenters, plumbers or electricians. It was a bit of a nightmare and it didn't really help me to keep the price of the house within bounds. In September, my parents came out to St. John's to visit us. We were not yet in the new house because of the delays so they started their visit by staying with Em Baird who made them very comfortable until they were able to move in with us.

My father was the youngest of six brothers and one sister who came in the middle of the family and he contended for years that, until he was married, he never knew that a chicken had anything but a neck. After the end of the First World War, he moved to Bowring and Company in New York, taking his wife and two young sons with him. We lived for about six years on Staten Island in a house called Bowcott in Dongan Hills, while he took the ferry each day to the office in 17 Battery Pl., New York. In 1922, my mother took us two boys back to England for a holiday of a number of weeks, so that she could give birth to what turned out to be my sister. She wanted her to be born in England and not in the United States. I remember that while we were over there staying with my paternal grandmother, both Norman and I developed whooping cough, which meant that Mother moved rapidly out of the way to stay with her own parents. They lived some blocks away and it was important not to incapacitate the soon-to-arrive infant. Everything passed off well and she, her two sons and her new daughter eventually returned to Staten Island. My father was a director of Bowring and Company and worked there until early 1926, when he manoeuvred himself back to England to join C.T. Bowring and Company in their London office. I suspect he initiated this transfer because he wanted to educate his children in England and did not want them brought up as Americans. I have always been thankful that he made that move and that we grew up and were educated and enjoyed our young life in England, which was really where we belonged.

When he returned to England and the London office, he was in command of something called the Works Control Department, which I have never clearly understood, but it seemed to be the department that was responsible for practically everything that didn't come under the heading of shipping or insurance. One of his particular activities, and the one for which Bowring Brothers in Newfoundland were always thankful, was the marketing in the U.K. or on the continent of the annual catch of sealskins, either furrier seals or hair seals. Working through a company called Elwyn Ingrams Limited, who were fur brokers and dealers, he established a fine market for the furrier skins and this resulted in superior returns. The sealskins that were suitable only for leather were more of a problem. In those days, the only tanning done of sealskins was what is known as vegetable tanning, which turned them into usable leather, but not leather that could be used by the shoemaking trade. Shoemakers wanted leather that was called chrome tanned, which was a process that used chemicals rather than natural oils, and it appeared that there were no tanners able

Mother with me, Sonia and Norman, c. 1922.

to do it. However, my father discovered a little tannery on the banks of the River Thames called William Duckworth Limited. After a certain amount of experimentation, they were able to chrome tan sealskin and make satisfactory shoe manufacturer's leather. This opened up an entirely new market that Cyril Bowring and a leather broker he employed in the Works Control Department developed for Bowring Brothers. The Duckworth who was running the tannery, which was soon to be owned by C.T. Bowring and Company, was not in the least surprised when my father was talking to him one day about a new wonder drug called penicillin, which came from mould. Mr. Duckworth said he'd known about the healing powers of mould for years, and his father before him. They all knew that if you cut a finger or drew blood somewhere, the cure was to stick your hand in and get a gob of the mould that was always on the back of the tanned leather and smear that into the cut. It cured it almost immediately. As far as he was concerned, that was penicillin, and although he didn't know what it was called, it worked.

Clara Bowring, c. 1935.

Cyril Bowring, 1948.

When my parents came for their visit, they had come from a still rationed and cheerless England, which had really not recovered very much from the end of the war. They landed in a place that, to them, looked like plenty of everything and good cheer and happiness surrounded them. They were also able to meet their two grandchildren for the first time. David, born in 1942, and a granddaughter, Paula, who had been born in November 1946 and was still quite small and not yet running around on her own two feet. They were fully occupied in admiring them, and my father said to Gig's mother, after he had seen Paula, that he had never in his life seen the perfect child but now he had in the shape of his granddaughter, Paula Bowring. My mother-in-law was highly entertained.

When they arrived, we were in the process of trying to get into our new house, which was not really anywhere near as complete as it should have been, so the house was full of painters, the odd plumber, an occasional electrician and a couple of carpenters. My father occupied his time down in the store, which fascinated him beyond belief and it wasn't long before he knew almost everybody who worked there and was busy acquiring their life histories. He excelled at making friends with people that he'd never heard of before. He was interested in what they did, where they lived, their families, how their children got on and it was unbelievable how much, after two or three weeks, he knew about almost everyone. Whereas my uncle, his brother and the next one older than him, had worked there since about 1910 and knew the managers as well as a lot of the employees by name, and greeted them whenever he met them, but actually knew very little about their private lives. It was so Cyril Bowring. He was right in the middle of the activities and became highly popular. Probably the most popular Bowring there's ever been. He did enjoy himself immensely. The shops, of course, were still in a certain amount of turmoil because we were in the first year of our new system of operating. A lot of people were doing a job that was quite different to what they had been doing before, but they were all enthusiastic and sales were good. On Christmas Eve or the day before, as we wound up for the climax of the Christmas trading and the biggest trading day of the year, the great hope was that we would reach sales of $10,000 for the store as a whole, excluding the grocery. By some miracle, we actually did it. There was great rejoicing and hoopla. And who should be there in the midst of it all, exhorting the troops, counting the pennies and all else – my father. I don't know what he was up to but he was right there leading the cheering section when we discovered that we had actually made it. By the time we had reached the Christmas trading period of 1947, Father had become part of the scenery in the store. He was, by nature, one of the great leaders of men and could make a real team work well together. The reason was that he truly loved his fellow man.

We had built our house on about 50 acres of partly cleared but mostly treed land, and we were about five miles away from the St. John's city limits, which meant we were way out in the country. We had planned to keep a cow or two and a horse for general purpose use and maybe, in the summer, we would fatten up a few pigs. We were also going to keep chickens on the top floor of a barn that we were in the process of building. So, to look after all this, I had employed a young man who was there every day, and Father, of course, couldn't resist helping with the building of the chicken runs and the roosts in the barn. At this stage of construction, these were reached by climbing up a ladder. Jim, my hired man, was up there one day with Father, as well as David, who was all of five years old. Suddenly there was a bit of a crash and David was found to have fallen through the hatch, missed the ladder and landed on the, fortunately, loose gravel soil at the bottom. His departure produced from Jim, a "Jesus, Mary and Joseph, he's disappeared!" My father scrambled down to get him but by the time he arrived on the ground floor, David was up and running and not a peep out of him.

We enjoyed having a bit of a hobby farm at the new house.

The horse was pressed into service after we had had a nice fall of snow and everything looked lovely and virgin white. Father offered to take Mother for a sleigh ride. We had a one-horse sleigh in which two people could sit side by side. It was not a side sleigh, but a proper Santa Claus sleigh. Agatha, the horse, was duly harnessed to the sleigh and her harness had a very musical and lovely sounding set of bells. Mother was hoisted into the sleigh and, with the old man in charge, off they went down the road on their little ride alongside Twenty Mile Pond. History has never related exactly how it happened, but he managed to tilt Mother out into the snow. It didn't do her any damage except to her dignity. He thought it was hilarious and he righted the sleigh, got her back in it and they trotted home in good order, but she wouldn't go out with him again.

On November 5th, we had celebrated Guy Fawkes Day and Paula's first birthday with a giant bonfire made from the scraps of wood left over from the construction period and two or three ship's rockets, which were the only fireworks that we could find available at the time. They went off with a considerable whoosh and spurred spectacular lights in the sky. After that came our first Christmas in our new house with my parents and my mother-in-law. It snowed quite a bit during the day, so that when it became time to take Em Baird home, there was a considerable depth of snow on the ground and my father and I mounted her on David's toboggan and towed her down the hill to where the car was parked down by

Agatha the horse, with Jim Butler, Paula, me and David, 1948.

the road. Once we had her on board, we drove her home to Monkstown Road in St. John's and the two of us came back without really too much trouble, although at one point my father had to get out and push a bit. It was a memorable Christmas and enjoyed by all. Early in January my parents returned by boat to England. They left in a pouring rain that removed the last vestige of snow in the St. John's area. Not to worry, however – we soon got plenty more. It was a memorable visit and, I think, from my father's point of view, it was one of the highlights of his life. He really enjoyed Newfoundland and its people.

January brought the time for stocktaking in the store and we expected a considerable shortage, meaning the difference between the value of the actual inventory that you count compared to the value of the book inventory that you think you should have. Since this was our first experience with the retail inventory method, we were not surprised when we did end up with a shortage – mostly due to error and theft. It was the beginning of a lengthy battle in controlling shortages every time we took a physical inventory. It's one of the nightmares of the retail business. Our overall performance of sales and the procurement of merchandise all went well and we were pleased with all we had achieved in the previous 12 months of conversion from one method to a more modern one, and it was to stand us in good stead from then on.

Our house, Broad Halfpenny, on Portugal Cove Road, c. 1965.
Photo: Paula Bowring

CHAPTER SIX
BECOMING CANADIAN

In 1948, Newfoundland was considerably exercised about determining its future, for with the end of the war, the country as it was then, had money in the bank and its debts were gone. The future, which was to be decided, was being debated between return to Responsible Government, the continuation of the Commission of Government which was in existence at the time, or the possibility of becoming the 10th province of Canada. All the possibilities for the future had their quite vociferous adherents and there was no lack of debate or noise about the whole process. The Commission of Government had set up what they called a National Convention, with members elected on the basis of the old ridings that had existed at the time of Responsible Government. These people gathered in the old Legislative Assembly and debated our future. It was a fairly noisy and obstreperous performance but it was clear that there would be a strong following for Responsible Government and, as time went on and we learned more about it, an equally strong preference for Confederation with Canada. The third possibility was the refuge of those who felt that Canada was an unknown quantity, but Responsible Government they had had enough of in years gone by. They had gotten rid of it and they didn't want it back so that group supported a continuation of the Commission of Government.

Newfoundland was essentially a failed dominion and, being insolvent and unable to borrow more in 1934, had asked the United Kingdom to take over the management of its affairs and provide local government. This resulted in what was called the Commission of Government, which was in force when I arrived in 1935 and lasted until Confederation in 1949. There were many causes for this financial disaster, one of which was the cost of maintaining an infantry regiment on the Western Front in the First World War, plus the immediate post-war slump when fish prices collapsed. This was coupled with political financial mismanagement and the world economic crash and the Depression from 1929 onwards. In 1935, the world was slowly emerging from the Depression and Newfoundland was moving in the same direction, even if the government was a rather peculiar establishment. It consisted of the Governor as chairman of the Commission and six commissioners, three of whom were civil servants from the U.K. and the other three were former Newfoundland politicians, all appointed by the Dominions Office. Each of the six commissioners acted as ministers of departments. There was a Commissioner of Finance, a Commissioner of Public Utilities, a Commissioner of Natural Resources, a Commissioner for Justice, a Commissioner for Home Affairs and a Commissioner for Health, which was a pretty heavy job in those days.

As might be expected, Commission of Government provided honest, if unimaginative, government and was answerable to the Dominions Office in London. The Dominions Office itself existed purely as a sort of contact point for the various dominions around the world and was not in itself, accustomed to very much in the way of direct government. The Commission might well have been better off if it dealt through the Colonial Office which was more accustomed to the ins and outs and ups and downs of direct government. The Commission suffered from the Dominions Office requirement that virtually everything the Commission wanted to do first had to be referred to London for approval, all of which was time-consuming and caused unnecessary delay and a good deal of quibbling about the cost of what was proposed. It seemed to have very little discretionary powers, particularly when it came to spending money and this was a handicap that the Commission suffered from for virtually the whole of its existence. It did manage to achieve stability in the country. The civil service was re-organized on a better basis and things functioned in a rather dull sort of way. Thanks to the coming of the Second World War and the prosperity that brought, chiefly through the construction and operation of the American army, navy and air force bases, the Commission was able to leave Newfoundland with a sizable sum of money in the bank. It was, in fact, something a little over $40 million and this at least gave the new provincial government a flying start. A great deal of it was later wasted in wildcat schemes, but that's another story.

I personally had no experience of Responsible Government, but from what I had heard about it and the people involved in the political process while it existed, I was certain in my own mind that I didn't want to see Newfoundland returned to that. The Commission of Government, on the other hand, was a fairly steady straightforward operation – dull and unimaginative, but reliable. However, the really good future seemed to me to lie in Confederation with Canada, which was a really magnificent country, doing well, always performed the way it should do in the world and with a population that was growing. It had a future that looked unlimited and it had the wit to recognize that it was not American, which was my own view. I remember one day walking back from some meeting or other with my uncle and as we walked along Water Street, I asked him what he thought about it and he said, "Well, I think that the only reliable, sensible future for Newfoundland lies in our becoming the 10th province of Canada, provided we can get a fair deal in the terms of union." Since that coincided with my own views, I decided at that point that's what I would vote for and that's what I did. However, most of the Water Street merchant group were against Confederation, with two notable exceptions, namely Sir Leonard Outerbridge of Harvey and Company and my Uncle Eric and I of Bowring Brothers.

Gig, on the other hand, had experienced Responsible Government and didn't want to go back to it. She rather liked the certainty, if not the unimaginative and rather plodding method of the Commission of Government, and in the first referendum held in 1948, voted for the Commission. The Commission came third in the voting with the other two virtually tied. In the second referendum, the Commission of Government was dropped from the possibilities and the vote was decided between Responsible Government or a Canadian province. Thank heavens the 10th province of Canada won the referendum, but in the interval there was a lot of shouting and yelling and name-calling and general rudeness, which we could have done without. Being Newfoundlanders and being argumentative, as well as witty, it was a bit of an uproar for a year or two.

Once we knew that Confederation with Canada was going to take place on the first of April, 1949, we thought that we had better find out in more detail exactly how the Canadian retail scene operated. Fred discovered in some trade magazine that a new organization had come into being called Allied Merchandisers of Canada, that it was headquartered in Montreal and had a membership that consisted of independent department stores in different cities across the country such as Halifax and Montreal, as well as the Ontario cities of Hamilton, Fort William and Ottawa. We discovered that they were simply trying to find a way that they could improve their operations and competitiveness, compared to stores that operated across the country on a chain basis. Since we were the first store to actually apply to join them, we were welcomed in with open arms, particularly as we seemed

Teaching David how to raise the Bowring house flag, c. 1949.

to be a bit of a freak. We weren't even Canadian. We were in an area that to them was totally strange; they really knew nothing about Newfoundland, but we spoke to them quite learnedly, we seemed to be reasonably well educated, we knew what retail was all about, we were a very old company, much older than any of the other members, and the pure novelty of having us included was, I think, what attracted them most. From our point of view, they were always most helpful, in the same way that Owen Owen and Duncan Norman had been helpful.

They went to considerable trouble to explain to us about how the Canadian retail scene operated and introduced us to various sales promotion and sales promotion credit granting schemes that became highly valuable to us in the years to come. It was a most enjoyable association, which lasted for several years until, for one reason or another or a change in circumstances, it was brought to a slow halt. Our group met twice a year, spring and fall, at two levels. One meeting would be designed for chairmen, owners or senior management, and the second meeting was for the various stores' merchandise managers so I attended one and Fred Ayre attended the other. Most of our meetings corresponded with the annual meeting of the Retail Council of Canada at which the Allied Merchandiser members used to sit and eat together while they attended the bigger trade convention. We became quite a clubby little group who carried on and reported our sales and all our results to one another. One of the chartered accountant companies collated all the merchandising information we provided and then put out results on an overall basis and, without naming names, classified how we stood in relation to one another. You knew your own number but that was all. Over the course of time, I visited each member's store and it really was highly helpful as an overall experience. I can't quantify how much it helped, but purely being in the presence of other people who had similar problems to your own was an advantage denied if you stood alone.

While all this was going on, Bowring Brothers' other activities were still proceeding. Salt fish was being bought and exported; cod oil was also taken in, tanked and shipped to the Canadian and U.S. markets, and the U.K. where it was mostly used for the purpose of tanning leather. Sealing was attempted, but on a small scale since we only had one ship left – the Eagle. In spite of her historic trip to the Antarctic during the war, she was still in fair shape, but it was shortly concluded that she had outlived her usefulness. She was ceremoniously towed out through the Narrows to the Cordelia Deeps and there, with her colours at the masthead, the sea-cocks were opened and she was allowed to sink to the bottom of the Atlantic, on which she had sailed for so many years. During the war we had lost the only really effective icebreaker – Imogene – as well as the Beothic, the Ranger and the Terra Nova. We had acquired a wooden sea-going tug from some American source – I think the U.S. Navy. It was built of wood because a wooden vessel was not susceptible to magnetic mines. She was equipped with greenheart sheathing and was thus able to go into the icefields. We had one small vessel built locally for the seal fishery and christened her Terra Nova II. She was diesel engine propelled but was really too small and did not have enough strength to do more than just putter around in loose ice and was not a great success at the seal fishery. We bought another, called the Ice Hunter, similar to the second Terra Nova, but again with too small a capacity, too low engine power and in turn, we sold her off. The Algerine underwent a conversion from being a sea-going tug to something suitable for the seal fishery. She was equipped with the most expensive Kuber-Bessemer diesel engine and altered to provide cargo space for seals and accommodation space for as many sealers as could be fitted in. She also was too small but had better power than the Terra Nova II and the Ice Hunter and she proceeded to the seal fishery for one or two years, but both the Algerine and the Terra Nova II found more lucrative employment in the summer months. They were chartered for two or three years to the Canadian Department of Transport, which, at the time, was conducting survey operations in northern waters where these two vessels were able to go. They were not very popular with the surveyors on these trips, however, because they lacked the comfortable accommodation that the men wished for, and they were too small, so they were only employed while the Department of Transport was building a suitable palace for its surveyors to live on in future years.

The cost of the Algerine's conversion was really outrageous and, unfortunately, at that time I was not in a position to do very much about it. We were not keeping up to date with how the cost was accumulating and when my uncle got wind of what was going on, it was really too late. Though he did have a fairly enduring row with the Newfoundland Dockyard which, after Confederation, was part of the Canadian National Railway system. We recovered a little bit of the outlay, but her cost was totally out of proportion to any cargo she might ever bring in. It was a total farce and another warning to me that Bowring Brothers needed a new chief accountant who could provide current operating figures and costs, rather than having to wait several months until the end of the financial year when the information was no longer useful. I was not only frustrated by the chief accountant's failure to post things quickly and promptly, but even more so by his failure to produce a figure for your information until he could ensure its accuracy to about 10 decimal places. I wasn't interested in decimal places, I was interested in total dollars, and quickly, so by a certain amount of guile, I had been able to persuade my uncle that the existing chief accountant, who in the past had saved my uncle's bacon, should be promoted sideways to become company secretary and take over the onerous duties of looking after the Company Seal, the minutes and matters of corporate history and so forth. We then asked C.T. Bowring and Company in London if they could find a well qualified chartered accountant who could take over the job of chief accountant and who had some experience with the mechanical accounting practices that were then becoming available. In due course, through their own auditors or the accounting field in London, they found one Len Wragg, who joined us later in 1948. He was a very competent accountant but not, unfortunately, a very good manager of people, and was inclined to get people's backs up. However, information began to come out of the books in a way that meant something to the managers concerned and we got a better grasp of how things were going in the shops, what they were doing, the mark-up we were achieving, the size of the inventories we were carrying, and so forth.

Through our connections with Allied Merchandisers of Canada and the new ideas about credit that we were learning, we had been indulging in a good deal of sales promotion based on the granting of new types of credit in the term-payment field and we had even started a scheme that we called "revolving credit." We were quite heavily involved financially in carrying this burden, which we did simply by borrowing from the bank. The size of the credit operation was really more than the existing credit manager could cope with and, therefore, he was retired and a new credit manager found who knew the retail credit picture quite well in St. John's. We also added an accountant to the credit department where the volume was growing by leaps and bounds, and this young man remained with the company to the end and achieved some quite miraculous results. The credit operation was totally changed. The money that had previously been put out financing wholesale accounts around the outports had now been changed to roughly the same amount of money, or maybe a little bit more, devoted to retail accounts. The great difference was that the new retail accounts were a revenue source on their own that covered the cost of borrowing plus the cost of labour to do the accounting and communication involved.

At the time of Confederation, Bowring Brothers and other similar businesses in St. John's, collectively known as the Water Street merchants, were, in essence, bankers to the colony. They supplied outport merchants all around the coast with their basic inventory supplies, all of this done on very long-term credit, mostly 12 months. Usually the debt would be paid, or part paid, in salt codfish, which the merchant had to take in and then run the risk of it deteriorating before it reached its designated market since it was a perishable commodity. One of the problems behind this system was the difference between the value of the merchandise provided on credit the day it was issued, and its value a year later when the credit was due; the inevitable discrepancy led to the Water Street merchants being called all the names under the sun. To be called a Water Street merchant was, in fact, an insult but they were the backbone of how the colony functioned economically. They could borrow money from Canadian banks and, in effect, lend it to the outport people who supplied the fishermen who caught the fish that ultimately, supposedly, paid the bills. This was still going on in the early days of Confederation but since we had separated our wholesale activities from the retail ones and they were now housed in a different building to the Water Street retail stores, we began to take a different view as to how things should operate in the future. Since Canada was now behind the commercial and industrial activities of Newfoundland and there was something solid that could be relied on for the future, and no fly-by-night Newfoundland government concerned about it, we thought that we could now establish our wholesale sales on more normal, reasonable short-term credit. As a result of this we decided that, in future, our wholesale sales would only be made on 30-day terms and we notified our outport wholesale customers of this change by letter. This effectively brought the wholesale business to a halt, for no outport merchant was going to contemplate paying on 30-day terms if he could possibly get credit elsewhere for longer, preferably 12 months. We thus exited the wholesale business in short order.

Another issue of Confederation, and probably one of the reasons so many other merchants were against it, related to the value of the stock in trade that we had for sale. Virtually everything we sold in Newfoundland had to be imported, and what we bought and sold came primarily from the United Kingdom, the United States or Canada. Regardless of where it came from, there were sizable customs duties paid on everything. That was how Newfoundland financed its government. Income tax was almost nominal but customs duties, which provided the revenue to the government, were colossal – 25 per cent ad valorem, and up, and this applied to virtually everything except fresh foodstuffs. So when you imported the merchandise, you immediately paid the duty to the customs department and then, when you counted the inventory, the value of it was based on the cost of the merchandise, the cost of the freight and insurance to get it to Newfoundland and the cost of the customs duty that you had paid on it. As of April 1, 1949, Canadian merchandise of all kinds came in and there was no duty on it as it was not being imported, it was moving to a new part of Canada. The duties on U.K. and U.S. products were very much reduced from what they had been and, in many cases, they were duty-free, too. Consequently, we were faced with the problem of how to treat the inventory that we had on the shelves on March 31st versus the inventory we brought in after April 1st. We decided, without too much debate, that the only sensible thing to do was to forget about the duty we had paid, price the merchandise at the current Canadian mainland price and take what would be a thumping loss at the end of the trading year. This we did, to the considerable annoyance of our competitors, who thought that they could recover the duty that they had paid on their stocks by having them sold before new merchandise started coming into the store. We had decided that that was much too risky a thing to do; the new merchandise would be arriving fairly quickly, even if it was just from mainland mail order suppliers, and we figured we would take our medicine and get on with the job. At the end of the year it showed that we had suffered a quite serious loss of potential profit as we gave away the duty paid on our stocks. However, it was good public relations; we could claim right away that we were now selling at Canadian prices: come on down and see how much you are going to save, and that, while it irritated the competitors, gave us a certain advantage and a bit of goodwill to boot.

In 1849, Bowring Brothers had become the first overseas agent of the Liverpool, London and Globe Insurance Co. Ltd. and the agency had continued until 1949 when the general manager of the Canadian headquarters came down to St. John's to present Bowring Brothers' Chairman with an antique inkstand as a memento of the centenary. At the time I joined Bowring Brothers, the agency was in full swing and operated by an insurance department that lived in the general office, and which consisted of two men and a woman. One of the men was the manager and chief source of insurance knowledge and the second man was a clerical worker. We had a considerable book of customers who insured mainly their houses and automobiles, and this continued throughout my period as chairman. I think that our agency was the one with the largest volume when I first became acquainted with it in the late 1930s. Liverpool, London and Globe underwrote all of Bowring Brothers' own insurance needs of fire and accident on vehicles as well. The company, by that time, was established in Canada and we reported to the Canadian office as opposed to the Liverpool office. In Canada, all insurance companies of that nature were members of what they called the Board of Fire Underwriters which, in effect, was a benign collective of all similar insurance companies in Canada who, between them, established rates to be charged for different kinds and levels of fire insurance and later, automobile insurance. They based their activities on the fact they really established and measured the risks involved. They had plans made of the main towns and cities and these showed clearly the class of construction that existed in different areas of each town; they had such a plan for St. John's and other smaller communities in Newfoundland. They argued that their knowledge of what risks existed to be covered justified them in setting rates that could only be described as monopolistic. Bowring

> THE NEWFOUNDLAND QUARTERLY.—42.
>
> ESTABLISHED 1836
>
> **When you require Insurance of any kind**
>
> Write, Phone or Wire
>
> **THE LIVERPOOL & LONDON & GLOBE**
>
> INSURANCE COMPANY, LIMITED.
>
> **BOWRING BROTHERS, LTD.,**
>
> Agents for Newfoundland.

Display ad for Bowring's insurance division, 1947.

Brothers, as the company holding the agency for Liverpool, London and Globe in Newfoundland, were members of the Newfoundland Board of Fire Underwriters, which operated in St. John's. As we developed our department store business, which we based on offering competitive prices with the implication that we would not be undersold by anybody, we found ourselves in a certain amount of turmoil in the years following Confederation when a new element entered the insurance scene. That new element took the form of local companies representing different syndicates at Lloyd's of London, quoting fire insurance rates below those quoted by the Board of Fire Underwriters to which Bowring Brothers were committed. This fact breached our lowest price policy and something had to be done about it.

The Newfoundland Board of Fire Underwriters used to hold annual meetings that took the form of a report to the members and included an election of officers consisting of a chairman, vice-chairman and a secretary general who was also the authority on matters of rates and physical assets being insured. He was also responsible for the inspection and maintenance of the sprinkler systems that existed in many members' and customers' businesses. When we ran into this problem of competitive rates in the early 1950s, Bowring Brothers attempted to get the Board of Fire Underwriters to recognize the problem and reassess rates in order to remain competitive with the Lloyd's rates that were being quoted by at least one or two of the local agents. This seemed to be impossible; nothing could shift the Newfoundland Board of Fire Underwriters from their established rates and their general routine – nothing short of a bomb was going to move them on this issue. Something had to be done about it so I set about looking for allies to act with me to bring the board into the modern world and we did make enough of a fuss that, at the next annual general meeting, when it became clear the fuss was going to be quite considerable, the chairman and vice-chairman decided not to run again and that left those positions open. The secretary general was an employee of the board and he was still in office, but it appeared that he was about to retire so that left an open field and into the opening I was thrust as the new chairman. One of my allies was the vice-chairman and the board of directors consisted of those who were on the side of the angels; that is, people who wanted lower rates. The Canadian Board of Insurance Underwriters was now fully aware of the situation in Newfoundland and knew that something was brewing and that they had better make some moves to try to keep the thing under control. The secretary of the board retired, so they sent a young man down from Montreal to be the new secretary general of the board. He made a fair amount of commotion and it looked as if things were going to move our way. We realized at Bowring's that it was unlikely we would reach the position that we hoped for – of being completely competitive. While this was going on, we were in touch with C.T. Bowring and Company Insurance Limited and, in particular, with one of the London directors, Ian Edward Bowring Skimming.

He suggested that we relinquish the agency of the Liverpool, London and Globe Insurance Company and substitute an agency for one of the Bowring companies called the English and American Insurance Company Limited, which was based in London and operated out of C.T. Bowring's own offices. Furthermore, we would be able to have the agency and be the general agents, which meant we would have the authority to set rates to compete with any Lloyd's rates that were offered in the province. This was exactly what we needed and so after a bit of writing to the Montreal office of Liverpool, London and Globe, we gave up this ancient agency and took on the new one. As far as I was concerned, the whole uproar was simply a matter of common sense. We had to be competitive and competitive we were going to be and competitive we became, but it was still Newfoundland and it was still St. John's where this all took place. I knew all the individuals concerned in the Newfoundland Board of Fire Underwriters, the chairman, the vice-chairman and the secretary general, and they were all, as far as I was concerned, elderly gents on the borderline of retirement, or beyond it. Of course, one of them, the secretary general, had to turn out to be my wife's uncle. I must say that fact didn't worry me, didn't worry Gig and it didn't worry her mother, who was the only person about whom I might have had some qualms, but the feeling of affection amongst them was not that great for various reasons and the change passed off without further ado. In point of fact, as time went by and we established branch offices for insurance in various parts of the island of Newfoundland, the department, with the English and American as the main underwriting company, plus the use of our connections with Lloyd's, brought the department along as a quite important part of the company's net profit for the year. The change we made because of our pricing policy turned out to be a good one in the overall picture and we never regretted it.

In March 1948, we welcomed our second daughter, Vivian, who distinguished herself at an early age. When it came time to bring her home from the hospital on April 3rd, we had had a fairly major snowstorm and we were only able to get her to the bottom of the driveway. At that point she was bundled up and carried by Gig; she made her grand entrance to her new home in the sleigh behind the ever faithful Agatha. I believe that was her last encounter with Agatha until she was about two, when she was found underneath the belly of the horse examining the necessary parts!

Our fourth and final addition to the family occurred in April 1949, when Norman, our only Canadian-born child, arrived. I was in England at the time, paying what I knew would be my last visit with my father, who was very ill. I was having a dreadful time trying to pluck up the courage to say my farewells when a cable arrived from my mother-in-law giving us the news of Norman's arrival. It really made it so much easier to leave Father

Gig with David, Vivian, Norman and Paula at the time of Norman's christening, 1949.

with such wonderfully joyous news, especially as we were going to name him after their son.

By the early 1950s, my Uncle Eric, back from his war responsibilities, remained as chairman but was not really active in Bowring Brothers' affairs except when Fred Ayre or I raised questions with him that needed answering. Though I was meant to be in charge of only the shops, he left it to me to sort out the insurance, among other things. We were still stuck in the salt codfish business and it took me some time and a good deal of persuasion to get us out of that business. It had always been unprofitable and we no longer needed it because we were not making sales to outport merchants; we were not extending that sort of credit and there were plenty of other people who could handle Newfoundland's fish business. We gradually withdrew and finally resigned our membership with the Newfoundland Association of Fish Exporters Limited. This had come into being by an Act of Parliament of the Commission of Government and it was established as the sole organization with the right to export salt codfish. This was to prevent the chaotic situation that arose when there were

10 or 15 or more exporters who couldn't agree on a price to be maintained with the general result being the ruin of the market. In fact, there was a tale in St. John's about a man who broke his leg running from the meeting where they had agreed on the export price, to get to the telephone so he could break the price and sell it for less.

In the late 1940s and around the time of Confederation, we were doing what today would be called rationalization. After we had absorbed the men who had left in 1940 to enlist in the Newfoundland Artillery Regiments back into the business, we found that we had too many men on the staff and not enough women, particularly considering that the complexion of the store itself had changed; we had more departments that were designed for and aimed at women, and rather less hardware, which would have required men. As a result of three or four layoffs of men, for whom we simply didn't have the employment available, we suddenly found ourselves in possession of a union, which had got itself certified. It wasn't a great surprise because we knew that the layoffs had caused a bit of a flutter and there had always been some kind of union presence from way back, almost from the time I started working in the store. Under the Confederation legislation, it had become possible to have the union certified after a vote amongst the employees. Previously, the union was very much a hit-and-miss business in terms of whether or not to believe them when they said they had a majority. In any event, it was of no great concern and we eventually met the delegation, negotiated an agreement for perhaps a year and carried on from there.

Each year produced new discussions, new demands, new denials, but the whole thing was peaceful, friendly and caused no distress, I think, on either side. The people who met us were not our own employees, but rather official negotiators from the union even though, as individuals, they worked in other stores along Water Street. In the negotiations, Fred Ayre and I represented Bowring's and there were usually three or four from the union: the president, the secretary and a couple of others co-opted to do the debating. It was usually quite amicable but occasionally there was a bit of a flare-up. I remember one occasion in which a man who worked at Parker and Monroe shoe store, which was a hotbed of unionism, remarked at the end of our negotiations that he certainly wouldn't want to work at Bowring's with an attitude such as I had towards them. I remember responding, "One day, Ron, you may find yourself in the position I'm in, that you are in charge of a store that you have to operate at a profit, and you will find that, if you have to negotiate with a union, you will probably argue in much the same way that I do." Anyway, that was the end of the debate. I was always interested in the fact that, after a very few years, he did exactly that; he left Parker and Monroe, established himself up at the top of Long's Hill and he was the boss. I think he did very well. I don't know whether he was unionized or not but I always hoped that he better understood what my point of view was, now that he was in charge of a store. Then there came a year of negotiations that occurred after the local union had affiliated itself with one of those American unions that call themselves International, even though they are purely American with a few Canadian members. On that occasion, there was the usual two or three from the Newfoundland union plus someone they had imported. I discovered later that he hailed from Chicago and was obviously planning to deliver the *coup demande* when it came to negotiating with Bowring Brothers; we were apparently reputed to be tough bargainers, which of course, we should be. Everything went peacefully to begin with and we operated in our normal way, but the union wasn't really getting very far in the discussions and so, I suppose, chummy from Chicago thought that it was time to level his big guns and demolish the opposition. He chimed in with what was nothing more than a thoroughly rude, quite inaccurate, disgraceful performance that should not take place in any actual negotiations of any kind. He really had nothing to say but was just, in plain English, bloody rude. I let him run down and he eventually ran out of breath. When he'd finished, I wasn't really too sure how to take it and what my reaction should be, and I found myself standing up from my chair, which was at one end of the table, and walking over towards my office window that looked out over the harbour – more to look at a bit of peace than anything else. While I was standing there, doing nothing, saying nothing, there was a pretty good hush over the rest of the collection and I suddenly heard Fred Ayre say, "Well, gentlemen, I think that ends our discussion for today." There was a scraping of chairs and people getting up and off they went. When they had gone, Fred and I exchanged views on how extraordinary it was for someone to think that that sort of behaviour was going to make any progress. It was quite beyond us and, apart from that, we laughed. We just sat back and waited for the union to reappear. I think "Chicago" was shipped off home on the plane that evening and a few days later, the union president rang up to ask if they might resume negotiations, to which we agreed. When they appeared this time, they started off with a very handsome apology for behaviour that they had brought with them the last time and said that they agreed, as we did, that that was not the way that they, or we, wanted to talk to one another, and peace reigned once more.

Some years later, when we were still pottering around with the union but had no serious items to negotiate, they sent us their proposed version for a new agreement as the old one was about to run out. They accompanied it with an invitation to discuss it at a time convenient for us. So, this time, we thought that instead of going the usual route of saying, "Yes, we'd be delighted to have negotiations with you, but come down to our office and do it here," we would accept their invitation and go to their offices. Why should we think they should have to come to us all the time? In due course, we turned up at their office on Water Street. Well, it was quite obvious that they'd had a good old cleanup before we arrived. I think they were so taken aback by the fact that we accepted their invitation to come there that the whole complexion changed – they were the hosts, we were the visitors, and normal politeness required that they show us into chairs with an "Are you quite comfortable there?" and "Would you like a cigarette?" or whatever. We sat down and started the negotiations, though there really was nothing very much to be said on either side. The only point over which we ever really had a disagreement was related to our closing day. We were determined that if the Shop Opening Hour legislation required a business to close on one day of the week, the day to close was Monday and no other. That gave our employees a two-day weekend and still allowed the store to be open on the Saturday, which was the busiest shopping day of the week. We would never move from that; it would have been suicidal to do so, but other stores, apparently, were quite happy to close on other days of the week and the union used to try to convince us to close on Wednesdays, which certainly didn't suit us. They realized that we would never, ever agree to anything that involved closing on any day other than Monday. We used to agree to disagree on that one. After a very pleasant little evening in their headquarters, and the work being done, Fred and I departed for home. Shortly after, we received a letter from the union saying that they didn't actually have a majority of our employees any longer, and I suspect they hadn't had them for quite a long time, and would we kindly apply to the Labour Relations authorities asking for them to be decertified. I think that having to deal with us was embarrassing to them in relation to dealing with other stores. We were so absolutely determined about the Monday closing that it handicapped their negotiations elsewhere. That meeting was an eye-opener as to what difference it makes when you're the host or you're the guest. It changes the whole tone of the conversation, the whole tone in which everything happens – very interesting. I wonder how many employers have actually acted on that basis. I suppose for most of the major operations in the really big companies with huge numbers of employees, the negotiations take place in neutral areas such as hotel rooms. Anyway, we were then clear of unions for the rest of my career.

During the second half of 1947 and in 1948, in what might be described as the department store era, we were getting encouraging sales out of the existing space that we had available. The sales promotion and display department, established by Fred Ayre and under his ever skilful guidance, was producing more than our actual merchandise assortment might justify, but nevertheless, we were getting the sales and we continued to turn as many square feet of warehouse and office space into selling space; but we were rapidly running out of useful gains in this way. We were making steady progress at improving our merchandise assortments, and the buyers, who were all newly appointed, were becoming more skilled and better acquainted with important suppliers.

In the early 1950s, sales continued to boom and we ploughed ahead with Confederation behind us and adapted to our new environment with a degree of success that made us think about the future. There really was not much more we could do with the available space on Water Street to give us more sales floor. At this time, our contact with the parent company in England was still through Edgar R. Bowring, Jr., who was established in the Liverpool office and who, of course, had spent some 16 years in Newfoundland with Bowring Brothers in the 1920s up to the late '30s. He paid us periodic visits in the summer, possibly every other year, theoretically on an inspection trip or something described in that form. In fact, it was a nice old holiday for him to come out to Newfoundland where he had many friends and could have a nice old jollification with them. Unfortunately, he always had a rather negative outlook and expected any changes we made to produce unsatisfactory results. He was not a great spender of capital, while we, on the other hand, were spending money fairly freely on the improvements to the store and the creation of more retail space. We showed him what we couldn't avoid showing him, but we never went out of our way to demonstrate anything that he might have missed on his own. It was far quicker to leave him in ignorance than it was to debate the whole issue all over again and we weren't going to stop it anyway. I remember at some time around this period when I was visiting with Duncan Norman of Owen Owen in Liverpool, I complained about Edgar's negative attitude to any sort of change or what I considered improvement. Duncan's reply was rather typically Duncan: "Well, you've got to remember, every business probably requires a set of brakes." I must admit that's what Edgar was. However, he was a rather nice man and in the end, he never really caused us any difficulties.

Our final effort in creating new space at Water Street was the addition of a very successful cafeteria, the Captain's Cabin, in an area that had originally been used for salt codfish storage. It was right at the back of the building, fronting on the harbour and had a good view through a large plate glass window that had been installed there. We found a most wonderful woman to take charge of it – Angela Abbott. She really made her mark establishing our restaurant in St. John's. Known as the Captain, Angela ran one of the most attractive, efficient and best food cafeterias in St. John's. There was an amusing incident early in its establishment. I think it was probably the first of its kind in St. John's and, at the time, the Lieutenant Governor, Sir Leonard Outerbridge, who was a good friend of my uncle, decided that he and his wife, with our agreement, would make a visit to the cafeteria and see how it was set up and operated. All the panoply of a Vice-Regal visit was set up and Sir Leonard and his wife duly arrived and were escorted, not only into the cafeteria, but into the background parts where food was prepared and where dishes were washed by a very fancy machine, the likes of which I had never seen, but which could wash and dry dishes at quite a phenomenal speed. At this point, the demonstration of all the mechanical gadgetry was being shown to the Outerbridges by a gentleman who was known as the equipment manager and who had been responsible for the installation of all these goodies.

In order to ensure a thorough demonstration of how the dishwasher worked, he actually interfered in its operation and shook in an excessive quantity of detergent and set the whole thing in motion. The next thing we knew soap suds, water and Lord knows what were pouring out of the machine all over the floor, and eventually got out into the cafeteria, down the stairs and created an unholy mess. It was much to His Honour's entertainment and delight to see something going adrift. We cleaned it all up and the Vice-Regal visit concluded in good form. We never had that trouble again as the equipment manager was not permitted, under pain of death, to put detergent in the dishwasher.

The question of credit had always been a major factor in business in Newfoundland, not only for the credit given to outport merchants on such a vast scale, but also the ordinary retail credit within St. John's itself, which was our major retail market. Most of the major stores had their own credit managers and seemed to operate on the basis that the knowledge they had was highly secret, not to be divulged to anybody, that only they knew the good risks and the bad ones. It seemed extraordinary, but a credit manager had no one to contact to find out whether Person A was a good credit risk and Person B was a poor one. There was absolutely no central pool of information and you weren't going to find out about it from your competitors. So when I had a visit from a marketing manager who represented the Associated Credit Bureaus of Canada, I immediately pricked up my ears and asked him about what the association did and how it worked and so forth. Naturally, I was just what he wanted, someone who would take an interest in the association and who might well be persuaded to take the lead in establishing a Credit Bureau in St. John's. One thing led to another and I agreed, telling him, "Leave the information that you have in your booklets and your letters and your papers with me and I will see what I can do to get something underway. If I make any sort of progress, I'll come back to you later on for further information and help in getting such a thing established," and with that he departed back to Toronto.

After I had thought about it a bit, I realized it was not much use to try to get it going by enlisting a large number of companies at the beginning. It would be much better to tackle the problem by interviewing five or six of the major retailers, then assess their positions and see if they were interested in working with me. If I found sufficient interest amongst that half dozen, then between us we could probably put up sufficient funds to hire a Credit Bureau manager, rent space for the bureau's office and buy whatever minimum amount of equipment would be needed. It seemed to me that the important part of the whole thing was to find the right manager. I first approached a man who was in a totally different line of business to Bowring Brothers, namely Fred Marshall of Marshall Motors Limited, who were the local agents for the Chrysler Company and who had a substantial garage on Water Street west. I felt sure that the automobile business must be quite heavily involved in credit operations, credit granting, and that he and his colleagues in the same line of business would probably have a good deal of valuable information about it. Marshall was a well-respected man in the community and if he backed the idea, it would carry weight with other people, so I made an appointment to visit him. By that time, I had acquired some idea of what initial costs we might incur before money came rolling in from people who were using the bureau. In discussing it with Fred Marshall, I suggested that if we could find 10 or 12 companies and get that group to put up, say $1,000 apiece to get the thing started, then with any luck, it should stand on its own feet from there on and pay its own way. Basically, he agreed with that and we also agreed that the best thing to do was to have the bureau owned by its members and not have it operating, as some of the bureaus do, as a private company with ownership held by one or two people – then it's just a moneymaking operation. If we had it as a co-op, with the current situation in St. John's, where nobody divulged any information to anybody else, we were more likely to have them enthused, or at least willing to give it a try, especially if they felt that nobody else was benefiting from the use of the information they were providing, but that we were all mutually benefiting from the pooled knowledge. On that basis, he agreed to tackle the other automobile dealers and I agreed to tackle the other department stores and any other major stores along Water Street that we felt would have extensive credit dealings.

That plan worked very well. A number of my competitors put up the same $1,000 each that Bowring Brothers did, as did Fred Marshall's automobile dealers. One or two came in at lesser amounts, they were smaller stores, and quite a number of small retail grocers joined in as well. We didn't ask them to put up anything very much in the way of capital, but we knew that they were a very valuable source of information, that they had local neighbourhood credit dealings and that they were their own credit managers as well as owners of the business and they had a lot of information that would provide us with basic background. So, with that all lined up, we then had to find a manager and that was a most critical decision. We advertised in *The Evening Telegram* to hire a manager for a Credit Bureau that was to be established in St. John's and asked applicants to write, giving their CV and any information that they felt pertinent, and send it to a box number in care of *The Evening Telegram*. After a suitable lapse of time, we collected the applications from *The Evening Telegram*. I was at home for a day or two, probably with a cold, and so Gig picked up the mail from the office and brought it out to the house. I remember sitting there with her in the room while I opened the letters, skimmed through them and putting them all in a heap. I know I said to her, "Here, there are quite a few applicants for the Credit Bureau. You probably know them all better than I do, which one of them would you pick?" It seemed to me there were two or three that were worth more than a glance, and so I gave her the heap of around 10 applications and she went through them one by one. Finally she said, "Oh, here, this is the one. This is the man you want." She remembered him from when she worked in the Bank of Montreal in the 1930s when he would appear as the messenger from, I think, Harvey and Company, bearing the paperwork for the bank. Even at that time, he was bright, cheerful, obviously enjoyed working and was never at a loss. Whatever questions might be put to him, he was decisive, and she thought that by now, which after all was about a dozen years later, he would make a first-class manager of a thing like a credit bureau. I always regarded Gig as a far better judge of character than I was. Based on the fact that she knew him and most of the others, whereas I did not, I decided that he was the one that I would recommend to our co-operative bureau members when we next met. He was selected and took over from then on.

We never had any trouble; we had plenty of capital to get the thing going. Steve French, the new manager, sold the idea of the business to all and sundry and we soon had a large membership. It was amazing how well the retail trade, whether it was ordinary household goods, automobiles, groceries or wherever retail credit was granted, all flocked in and suddenly found that pooling their knowledge was the best thing that had ever happened and that they could avoid bad debts and improve the standing of their current receivables. Finally, they had reached a sort of heaven and the bureau never looked back. The period I am talking about, of course, is an era before the days of credit cards – there were no Visa and Mastercard. There was American Express, but it was not used for ordinary retail credit; credit granting was strictly based on a company's own money being used, so it was highly important that it be done with as much knowledge as possible.

CHAPTER SEVEN
EXTENDING BRANCHES, CATCHING FIRE

With all available space at Water Street now devoted to the pure sales operation, our thoughts turned to the question of branches, as we felt we had plenty of room to grow. It may have got into our heads partly because one of the members of the Allied Merchandisers, the one in Fort William, Ontario (now Thunder Bay), had a main store in Fort William and moderate, but still useful miniature department store branches in industrial areas in the vicinity of Fort William, up to as much as a hundred or so miles to the east and north. They were successful, profitable and worth having, and could be handled by the buying organization at the main store in Fort William. I think this is what probably made us think about whether we could do something of a similar nature.

We started in a small way by finding a very modest little building that we could rent in Churchill Park, which was the retail shopping area of what was known as "the housing." This was a sizable development on the north side of St. John's that had been established soon after the war ended, and was a modern and well thought out new housing area for the city. We planned at first to operate it around the Goodrich Tire Company, whose products we represented in Newfoundland. They were developing small automotive stores and I remember making a trip to Kitchener to see how they did it and whether that would fit the picture in Churchill Park. In fact our branch wasn't very successful in that form and we quickly converted it into what you might call a local convenience store for housewares and hardware, which did not exist in that area. It was small but it did give us experience in branch operation, it couldn't get into much trouble, and it made a modest amount of money. About the same time, we acquired an existing business on Bell Island from a gentleman there who had run it for many years and who wanted to retire. It was a small local dry goods and grocery store, which catered to the mining community on Bell Island, where the iron ore mines had existed for many years. However, realizing that it was very likely they would not exist for much longer, we bought the business but leased the building, including a clause in the lease that should the mines on Bell Island close, our lease would come to an end. This did eventually happen but we were there for several years. It was a profitable little store and gave us a bit more experience. We had a grocery at Water Street and it was not much more difficult to take over the one on Bell Island and run that, plus the dry goods and hardware that were carried in the Bell Island store.

It was around this time that the parent company decided they would increase our capital by $500,000. They realized that because of the ships we had lost during the war, all of which were insured with Lloyd's in pounds sterling, we had lost a considerable amount of money because of the pound. When the vessels were insured, the pound was worth about $4.85 but we couldn't get the pounds out of England during the war and when we could get them, after the war, the pound was only worth $2.20. We took a serious loss that was none of our doing purely because of the inability to let us take our money out of the country at the time the ships were lost. Understandable from their point of view in wartime, but not very fair to those who were trying to run their business on a sound basis. This increase in capital took care of any loans we had at the bank at the time, and left us with something in hand. We began to seriously think about where we might establish something of big enough proportions to make a real difference. There were several possibilities. Newfoundland had two towns whose economies were based on paper making: Grand Falls and Corner Brook. There was a sizable town around the airport in Gander and, at that time, Gander was of extreme importance for transatlantic flights since there were no planes that had the fuel capacity to fly non-stop from, say, Montreal to London or from New York to London. All of them had to refuel in Gander and they had to do the same on the westward passage as well. Gander was known as the "Crossroads of the World" and had tremendous traffic in aircraft both day and night. It was certainly a 24-hour-a-day operation and a good-sized town had grown up around the airport. Corner Brook was probably the most prosperous area but we discovered that the only way of having a store in the town of Corner Brook proper was to buy an existing business, which did not appeal to us and we thought it would give us more trouble than starting a new store of our own. Gander did not have a clearly defined retail trading area and was too new a place to be properly organized. This led us to Grand Falls, a well-established paper-making town, and there we found that we would be welcome, provided we put the store on their High Street. So to Grand Falls we went and plans were drawn up for a new building and overall arrangements made for what we would put in it, what departments, what personnel we would require, and who was to be the manager.

    At that time, what is now the Trans-Canada Highway was being built and most of it was in pretty rough condition, so that to go from St. John's to Gander was a lengthy and not very comfortable trip and not very good for one's vehicle, either. We would fly to Gander, rent a car there and drive on a not too bad road to Grand Falls, and do the reverse coming back. So Grand Falls was built, provided with stock, personnel and a manager, whom we sent from Water Street. This also meant that we had to provide a manager's house, which increased the investment. Grand Falls opened in 1958, with a full fanfare of trumpets and welcoming noises and help from the Anglo-Newfoundland Development Company management, and we really felt quite at home from the beginning. Grand Falls was our first branch well away from Water Street that could not be visited for short hops or part of a day. It meant one had to plan for two or three days to get out there, do what you wanted to do and return to Water Street. The experience gained here acted as part of our learning process in handling branches. The store started reasonably well, although not quite up to expectations, but we always managed to make a profit at the Grand Falls trading level and worked away at it for the number of years that we owned the store. It never lived up to our hopes and became, in the end, something that we would rather do without.

One day in 1958, Fred Ayre and I were standing in my office discussing nothing in particular, and doing it very well, when my secretary came through the door bearing the morning's mail, which she had opened. Instead of putting it on my desk, she handed it to me. I started to run through it casually while still carrying on the conversation with Fred. I stopped suddenly and I said to him, "Well, here's a new one. What would you think of this?" and read out to him what was on the piece of paper in my hand. It was an invitation from the Department of Trans-

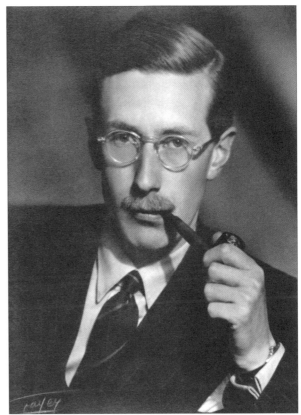

Myself, c. 1953. *Photo: Tooton's*

portation in Ottawa asking if Bowring Brothers would like to tender for the gift shop space in the new Gander Airport terminal, which was under construction. I believe his first comment, after he had absorbed what I read out, was, "Well, we could hardly do worse than the people who are there now," and with that I had to agree. Gander Airport terminal was a hodgepodge of buildings, previously built for wartime use, and they had been converted both to a passenger terminal and luggage distribution point. Some of the buildings had been converted to rather ordinary hotel rooms and in amongst it all there was a restaurant and bar that was open 24 hours a day, 365 days a year. While the planes were on the ground being serviced and refuelled, passengers were normally allowed off to stretch their legs and have a look at the local scenery, do a little shopping or have a drink or even a meal while they waited. The flight across the Atlantic had taken at least seven or possibly eight hours, and all passengers were more than ready to climb out of the plane and stretch their legs, even for a brief period. Gander terminal, therefore, had a very sizeable number of passengers moving through it every day of the week.

When we turned to discussing the question of whether we should make a bid to the Department of Transport, we realized that we already made stops in Gander because of the store in Grand Falls, which we had to visit from time to time for management purposes. Thus having to go to Gander to look after the affairs of a store there would not add to the expenses. We could do it as part of a trip to Grand Falls and, as Fred had said, we felt sure we could do a better job than what was in the old terminal. The new Department of Transport terminal, properly organized and established, was due to open in 1959, so there was roughly a 12-month period in which we could get ourselves organized. I offered to get in touch with Jim McGrath, who was the member for St. John's East in the Diefenbaker government, and ask him if he could ascertain the sort of percentage rent the department expected to obtain for this type of lease. We thought that three per cent of sales would be about enough to pay by way of rent. We were not going to go overboard as we had no idea what we might achieve with such a store, and it was going to be quite small even though it wouls be open 24 hours every single day. We realized that we would have to run three shifts, all of which would add to the expense. Our whole discussion did not take very long and we ultimately decided that, provided the three per cent rental figure sounded reasonable after our consultation with Ottawa, we would make a firm bid for the gift shop in the new Gander Airport terminal building. I don't believe that either of us gave it another thought from there on. We certainly did not realize that we had just made the most momentous decision of our entire business careers.

Once I had discovered that the three per cent rate sounded about right, we filled in the tender form and mailed it off to the address in Ottawa and both Fred and I then completely forgot about it. Several weeks later, a letter arrived from the Department of Transportation (DOT) in Ottawa and, believe it or not, we had won the jackpot. It actually took us a bit to remember what it was we had succeeded in winning – the Gander terminal gift shop. It fit into our overall plans nicely. It wasn't going to be a very expensive venture but we realized that we didn't have too much time to get things organized in the way of finding a manager, finding the staff, planning the layout, ordering and installing the fixtures and, finally, and most importantly, sorting out what merchandise we were going to offer in this new acquisition. We advertised in the Gander papers and, shortly afterwards, we acquired a manager from the town who came into St. John's to discuss how we were going to go about the whole thing. He returned to Gander to line up the necessary staff, knowing that the store would be open 24 hours a day, which, of course was the normal way that things worked in Gander. The airport never closed, and the people who worked there – and that was the main source of employment – were all accustomed to working in three eight-hour shifts, every day of the week. So lining up the sales staff for the store was not as difficult as you might think. After we had decided on the type of merchandise that we would offer in the store, we were then

then Vancouver in 1972. So now Bowring's had three regional managers: David in Ontario, Bruce in the west and a fellow named Jerry Belair in Quebec. Bruce was responsible for opening those 24 stores in 24 months in Western Canada, including ones in Edmonton and Calgary on the same day! We were then planning to transfer Bruce to Chicago in 1974 as we had begun to open stores in the U.S. as well, but these plans were cancelled at the last minute and we sent him back to Ontario instead. By the time David and Bruce left Bowring's in the mid-1970s, there were 96 stores, most of which they had opened.

When Bowring Brothers entered the U.S. with the Little Shops, it created a certain amount of excitement. The first shop was opened in New Jersey, at a place called Paramus and it proved an almost instant success, which was not surprising since it was managed by the most successful Little Shop manager that we had ever employed, Amy Howell, and she was determined that this one was going to work from the word go. When I retired at the end of 1977, I believe we had 14 stores in the U.S., scattered all over the place, which in itself was a mistake, because we could have put the 14 stores all in one state if we'd put our mind to it. Each time that we moved into a new state it was just as difficult as if we were moving into another foreign country, so different were the regulations, taxation and reporting requirements. It nearly drove our accounting staff mad. We had planned to open even more stores in the U.S. but the business model simply did not work. The ideal was to build a store for $100,000 and fill it with $100,000 worth of merchandise, but the capital cost of building in the American malls was roughly double that in Canada. Canadian mall owners provided more for their tenants, such as concrete floors, air conditioning, store fronts, sign boxes, etc. In some U.S. malls, we had to pay for the pouring of our own concrete and for the installation of our own air conditioning system. We eventually learned that it was better to replace an original tenant than to go into a brand new mall.

I remember one U.S. store opening that I attended in St. Louis, which is an extraordinary place. St. Louis is quite a small city, but the greater St. Louis area consists of about 14 different municipalities, each with its own mayor and council. To the outsider this looks most peculiar, but they developed, in one of their municipalities, an architecturally lovely mall in which a Bowring Little Shop appeared, sitting, as we usually did, right outside the main entrance of the most prestigious department store in the mall – Neiman Marcus. On the opening day, Stanley Marcus came out into the mall from his own store to inspect his neighbours and the first store he met was the Bowring Little Shop. He went into the store, walked around, chatted to the staff, left and went straight back into the Neiman Marcus store. He then reappeared, accompanied by all his department managers and stood outside the Bowring shop and said to them, "Now, look at this store. This is what a store should look like." It was probably one of our greatest compliments and caused a considerable stir amongst the Bowring people present. In 1975, with Angela Cantwell the general manager at Water Street and in charge of the insurance department, and with the Little Shops in full flight across Canada and in the U.S., Bowring Brothers achieved a record profit, passing the $1,000,000 mark for the first time.

At some point around 1970, we were offered a business having to do with a special kind of treatment of cod oil, which produced a fluid that had proved effective in preventing the deaths of chickens. The owner of the process and the business that produced it in St. John's was anxious to retire and, since we had premises on the south side of St. John's that could easily be utilized for the process, he wondered whether Bowring Brothers would be interested in buying the business from him. The offer was made to a director on our board who, in the past, had looked after all the sealing, fishery and related activities and who was the logical person for the process owner to approach. It was duly presented to our board at their next meeting, without particular recommendation as to whether we should do it or not, but more to sound out the overall view. It was very clearly established that we did not want to buy the business, nor did we want to get mixed up in that sort of processing and exporting, however successful the business might have been – we were out of fishery-related ventures and we intended to remain out and that was a unanimous board decision. However, and here is where we made the great error, the director concerned asked us if it would it be all right if he forwarded the information to C.T. Bowring and Company in order to help the man who presently owned the process. Our parent company had a business in Liverpool called C.T. Bowring and Company Fish Oils Limited who might well be interested in it. We foolishly said that none of us had any objection to him doing that and there the matter rested.

The information was sent to C.T. Bowring and Company Fish Oils Limited and we proceeded to forget about it. But that was not the end of the matter. They were, unfortunately, only too interested in buying the business and using our Southside Premises for doing the processing. That was all right as far as we were concerned, except that the United Kingdom still suffered from exchange control activities and could not obtain the Canadian dollars needed to buy the business without a great tedious preamble and fuss and bother with the U.K. exchange control authorities. The U.K. was still wallowing in misery left over from the end of the Second World War. The country had had a succession of ineffective and moribund governments, alternating between Labour and Conservative, mostly Labour, where trade unions reigned supreme and the general attitude there was one of hopelessness and a lack of initiative.

The trade unions seemed to run the country until 1979 when Mrs. Margaret Thatcher became the prime minister with her housekeeping broom and swept the whole lot of them out of the House. She put the country back on a constructive basis where people could get on with things and earn money and generally make life worth living. But at the time of this fish oil business, the U.K. was still back in the dark ages of hopelessness. This resulted in the one and only bit of direct interference in the affairs of Bowring Brothers that I had encountered in my entire career. The way we operated the overall connection with the parent company was that I, as chairman of Bowring Brothers, reported to one of the directors on the board of C.T. Bowring and Company. In this case, the one that I reported to, Edgar Rennie Harvey Bowring, had cut his eye teeth in the fish oils business, the very company to which we had sent the information about this cod oil business. His sympathies lay primarily, I think, with the fish oils company and he saw an opportunity to oblige them. Even though he knew he wouldn't get the dollars that he needed, he knew where the dollars were, and therefore he found it simple enough to write to me to say that the parent company would like Bowring Brothers to put up the money required to buy the cod oil business and provide the operating capital. Fair enough, we could do that. We were well in with the bank; in fact, we had a little cash on hand at the time, and we bought the business on their behalf and hoped that they would make a success of it. Unfortunately, it was a disaster from the word go, nothing but a drain on our funds, and we found it very irritating.

In the middle of this undesirable activity, the director who had originally brought the subject up with Bowring Brothers died and we were left with it. It did nothing but lose money because the production could never get up to what was needed to satisfy the American buyer of the medicinal fluid. Eventually, I visited the Newfoundland minister of Fisheries to see if I could improve the supply of cod livers that we needed to fulfil the orders that were coming in. The result of this visit, and his investigation plus his officials', was that if I got every last cod liver that was landed in Newfoundland in a given year, I would still not have enough to satisfy the requirements of the process – that seemed to me to pretty well answer the question of the viability of the operation. The business was sold to the man whom we had installed as manager, and he was told to go ahead and do what he could with it on his own account – we were having no more to do with it.

It was a perfect example of interference without knowing anything about the circumstances or the problems or even proper research into the viability of the business that was being bought. I found it very annoying at the time, and even thinking about it now makes me quite hot under the collar.

The 200th anniversary of the birth of Benjamin Bowring was celebrated in 1978 at a very sizable lunch organized by the chairman of C.T. Bowring and Company and held in London for a vast number of members of the family. I wasn't there; I was busy endeavouring to develop a hog farm in Ontario with my son David, but my mother attended and was greatly entertained to be acclaimed as the oldest member of the family who was present. In fact, at 91, she was probably the oldest one in existence. She met a great many relations she hadn't seen for years and a happy and jolly party was the result of the gathering. I was sorry to have missed it.

Just as I was retiring, things were starting to unwind at C.T. Bowring and Company. In the 1960s, Ian Skimming had been busy acquiring other businesses, and in 1964, the first one came in the shape of a major finance company, followed shortly thereafter by a merchant bank. The finance company brought with it a Caterpillar dealership for the United Kingdom, and there were assorted insurance brokers acquired as well. After all these acquisitions, peculiar names and faces began appearing on various group boards, which did not go down particularly well with some of the older hands. Nevertheless, that was modern life and there we were.

Early in the 1970s, Ian Skimming died very suddenly and this left a difficult situation for his successor, Edgar R.H. Bowring, a cousin of mine, not quite a year older than me, but who had been on the board of C.T. Bowring and Company for a relatively short time. He was a solicitor who had practised that profession all his working life until he joined CTB Insurance, still working in a legal capacity. As chairman, he then was stuck with this queer variety of activities and companies that really only Ian could understand and could handle in whatever way it was that he had intended. Edgar certainly had not given a great deal of thought to the future but now, as Chairman, he was stuck with it.

At some time during the 1970s, there had been what one might call a financial crisis having to do with the financial company that C.T. Bowring and Company had acquired in the Skimming era of growth. I personally never knew much about it, but it caused a bit of a fright at the time and, I think, induced a good many family shareholders to sell their shares and get out of the way for such a thing had never happened in the history of the company. It was all sorted out in the end. It caused Edgar Bowring a good deal of trouble and I have a strong feeling that the combination of new companies acquired during the Skimming regime that were totally unrelated to any other Bowring activities, plus the financial crisis must have sown the seed in Marsh & McLennan's mind that it was time to act. Marsh & McLennan was a major U.S. insurance firm that wanted to be a member of Lloyd's but they needed to own a British company for that to happen. And now here was the company through whom they operated in the London insurance market showing signs of, perhaps, senility, and they very likely decided that, before the C.T. Bowring and Company Insurance Limited goes under, we had better make a bid for the whole package and get rid of these outside influences that seem to be having an undesirable effect on the overall operation. Who knows? It makes the most likely explanation that I can think of and, with that, in the early 1980s came the bid to buy the C.T. Bowring and Company shares – a sad end to what had been a brilliant business. At the time the Marsh & McLennan bid was made, the family shareholding was down to a very low level, and I later learned that the biggest single shareholder of C.T. Bowring and Company Limited was the British Railways Pension Board and they would rather like to accept the offer so that was the end of the debate.

In the final result, Bowring Brothers and other non-insurance divisions were sold off but Bowring Brothers kept operating in the retail business under its own name, though it had multiple owners over the years. Consequently, the original company, Bowring Brothers Limited, disappeared from St. John's for a time.

When a brand new store was opened in St. John's in 2004, the new owners allowed me to cut a ceremonial ribbon at the opening, with the mayor of St. John's in attendance and holding one end of the ribbon. It was a great and hilarious party that set the shop underway. The opening occurred during an October blizzard but that didn't dampen the attendance and, on the morning of October 30th, 2004, Bowring Brothers reappeared in St. John's, Newfoundland,

Derrick Bowring, c. 2000.

to be greeted by a vast pile of customers who gave them one of the biggest openings of any Little Shop. This astonished everybody who wasn't familiar with it before. The manager of the store told me a few days later, when I visited the store as a customer, that they had experienced a tremendous welcome from the public. Half the people that came in told them, "Well, thank goodness you're back, I've missed you," and the other half said, "Well, when I first started to work, that's where I went, 'Down to Bowring's!'"

Looking back at it all, I had joined Bowring Brothers in 1935 to be the first Bowring to know anything about the shops. By the time I retired, we had shops galore, from Atlantic to Pacific in Canada and about 14 in the United States – all profitable. I never once regretted my decision to board a ship and make a life in Newfoundland. Like my father, I developed a tremendous love for this island and a great affection for its people.

EPILOGUE

It is a rare privilege for a granddaughter to edit her grandfather's memoir, to gain insight into a life fully lived before you had even arrived on the scene. Family history and our Newfoundland heritage has been a rich part of our upbringing, and even though my brothers and I did not grow up in Newfoundland, our parents, both native Newfoundlanders, made a point of exposing us to the culture of their homeland, as that's what it was when they were born – not yet a province of Canada. The history, songs, landscape, language and foods of Newfoundland always had a presence in our home and our maternal grandmother dutifully sent a box at Christmas containing Purity Kisses, Mount Scio savoury and hard biscuits for fish and brewis.

Because we lived in rural Ontario, there were only a handful of years in the late 1970s when our Bowring grandparents lived nearby, but the memories of those years are vivid. There were many days when we were delivered there after school while our parents worked on the farm; Granny would give us a snack of dark-chocolate digestive cookies or toasted English muffins with jam and butter, along with a glass of cranberry juice. After Sunday dinners, we watched *The Muppet Show* with Grampy, who laughed the hardest. He would amuse us for ages with his imitation of chickens clucking or with some English rhyme from his childhood: "Willy in an awful curse, threw the coffee pot at nurse. When it hit her on the nose, Mother said, 'How straight he throws.'" I learned to play piano in their home using the piano my Granny, Gig Bowring, purchased with the wartime reparation funds she received, having been torpedoed.

Granny and Grampy always disappeared to Burnside, Bonavista Bay, in the summers – forced out by Ontario's extreme heat and humidity. After a few years in Ontario, they retreated to Newfoundland permanently, spending their retirement years in Topsail and Burnside. Their daughter, Vivian, who had become a nurse, raised her own family next door and was on hand when Granny's, and later Grampy's, health declined. Granny/Gig died in 1990 but Grampy/Derrick remained at the house in Topsail until his own death on December 10, 2009. They saw the births of 11 grandchildren and Grampy was there for the arrivals of 11 great-grandchildren (and one more was on the way at the time of his death). They had a flagpole at Burnside and he had a flag for every province or country where their grandchildren had been born; changing the flag during visits to Burnside was an important ritual for all of the grandchildren. I remember him as a very active grandparent: horsing around with us, sailing, gardening, walking and, most importantly, enjoying Newfoundland and its people. Had he lived a little longer, he would have been pleased to hear the news that the Schmidt Ocean Institute had accidentally found the wreck of the Terra Nova in Arctic waters during routine testing of their multibeam mapping echosounders. He would have no doubt noted that she was found in the Arctic exactly a century after she had taken Scott to the Antarctic.

Every letter he ever wrote to me was signed, "Your ever loving Grampy." Despite an outlook that was conservative in the mind of a grandchild, and an exterior that was frequently proper and sometimes cantankerous, he was always full of good humour and good stories and somehow I always knew that he was our "ever loving Grampy." We are grateful to have his story recorded for all his descendants.

As editor, I am grateful for the contributions of David Bowring, Norman Bowring, Robert Pallard, Vivian Pallard, Michael Ripley, Bruce Templeton and Paula Templeton, whose efforts ensured that this story would be shared with many generations.

Amy Bowring, 2014

BIOS

Born in Liverpool, Derrick Bowring (1916-2009) arrived in St. John's in 1935 to join Bowring Brothers Ltd. and learn the retail side of the family business. With Fred Ayre, he expanded Bowring's retail business into iconic gift shops across Canada. When he retired in 1977, he was chairman of the board of directors.

Amy Bowring is the Director of Collections and Research at Canada's national dance archives, Dance Collection Danse, and is an instructor at Ryerson University. In the field of Canadian dance history, she has curated exhibitions, published articles and lectured widely. She is the granddaughter of Derrick Bowring.

Photo: Travis Allison